Differentiating
Instruction
With Centers

in the Gifted Classroom

Differentiating Instruction With Centers

K-8

in the Gifted Classroom

Edited by
Julia Link Roberts, Ed.D.,
& Julia Roberts Boggess

PRUFROCK PRESS INC.
WACO, TEXAS

Library of Congress Cataloging-in-Publication Data

Differentiating instruction with centers in the gifted classroom / [edited] by Julia Link Roberts & Julia Roberts Boggess.
   p. cm.
 ISBN 978-1-59363-839-9 (pbk.)
1. Gifted children--Education. 2. Individualized instruction. I. Roberts, Julia L. (Julia Link) II. Boggess, Julia Roberts, 1972-
 LC3993.D54 2012
 371.95--dc23
                    2011044720

Edited by Lacy Compton

Cover and layout design by Raquel Trevino

ISBN-13: 978-1-59363-839-9

At the time of this book's publication, all facts and figures cited are the most current available. All telephone numbers, addresses, and websites URLs are accurate and active. All publications, organizations, websites, and other resources exist as described in the book, and all have been verified. The editors and Prufrock Press Inc. make no warranty or guarantee concerning the information and materials given out by organizations or content found at websites, and we are not responsible for any changes that occur after this book's publication. If you find an error, please contact Prufrock Press Inc.

Prufrock Press Inc.
P.O. Box 8813
Waco, TX 76714-8813
Phone: (800) 998-2208
Fax: (800) 240-0333
http://www.prufrock.com

DEDICATION

This book is dedicated to all teachers who differentiate in their classrooms to allow all children to make continuous progress, which requires lifting the lid off of learning. We also dedicate this book to teacher educators who prepare future teachers to differentiate based on readiness, interests, and learning profiles. The goal, of course, is for all children to thrive in school—not just survive. The phrase *all children* includes those who are gifted and talented—students who must not be overlooked if they and our communities, states, and nation are to thrive.

ACKNOWLEDGMENTS

A topic such as differentiating using centers and agendas requires specialists in various content areas in order to make the examples relevant. We value the authors of the chapters who have provided examples in each of the core content areas—Tracy Inman, language arts; Jana Kirchner, social studies; Martha Day, science; Janet Tassell, mathematics; and Jan Lanham, the arts.

A special thank you is extended to Gail Hiles, who provided important assistance with the figures and tables.

Of course, we appreciate our readers who work to differentiate in their classrooms. Teachers who differentiate make school a place in which all children and young people engage in learning. What an important concept that is—everyone learning each day he or she is in school. Such a classroom develops lifelong learners.

TABLE OF CONTENTS

Chapter 1

Getting Started Differentiating With Centers

Julia Link Roberts and Julia Roberts Boggess

Education must be increasingly concerned about the fullest development of all children and youth, and it will be the responsibility of the schools to seek learning conditions which will enable each individual to reach the highest level of learning possible.
—Benjamin Bloom

Learning centers provide opportunities for elementary and middle school teachers to tailor instruction so that all students learn about a particular topic or concept while engaging in learning experiences matched to their levels of readiness, interests, and/or learning profile. All teachers know their students differ considerably in their readiness to learn a particular topic as well as in their interests related to that topic of study. In addition, students differ in their learning preferences. This book presents ideas for differentiating in general and for differentiating with learning centers specifically.

This book introduces strategies to plan and implement centers so that all children learn on an ongoing basis and includes instructional management strategies to make these centers work effectively. There are ideas for differentiating through learning centers for students in kindergarten through grade 8, and different chapters focus on specific content areas—language arts, social studies, science, mathematics, and the arts. The chapter on the arts provides a multidisciplinary approach to differentiation.

CENTERS AND AGENDAS: WHAT ARE THEY?

A learning center is a hub of learning. The term *center* as used in education denotes a place in the classroom where students go to engage in learning in any subject area or in a multidisciplinary study. The goal is to engage students in minds-on learning—hands-on learning, too, where that is appropriate. In the center, students find instructions and resources for learning experiences designed for individual students or small groups of students. The center is likely the place to locate materials needed for implementing projects. Instructions in the center may be written or recorded. The center is usually the place where the student and/or students work on the learning assignments.

Centers are created for a variety of purposes. A center can be permanent in the classroom. One example would be an editing center. Throughout the year there would be a need to have the tools used when editing, including space for a partner to provide feedback as a peer editor. Centers can be set up for reading, including listening stations and comfortable places to read. Centers also can be planned for differentiated learning experiences. These centers will change as the units of study evolve. The purpose of any center is to facilitate and enhance learning.

If the center is used for students to pick up the differentiated assignments or there is no space in the room for centers, the term *agenda* can be used. *Merriam-Webster's Collegiate Dictionary* defines agenda as "a list or outline of things to be considered or done." Where space is a problem in the classroom, agendas can provide instructions for learning in the much the same way that centers do, and then students can gather in another location in the classroom or elsewhere in the school as they engage in the learning experience. Agendas provide the written instructions that can be picked up from a specific location in the room or distributed to individual students. They can designate what must be done, with whom, and by when. It is logistics that separate centers from agendas and not the assignments themselves.

Centers and agendas provide ways to organize differentiated assignments within a classroom. The very term *centers* or *center time* suggests that students will be engaged in learning in a variety of ways and in different locations within the classroom. The key item, of course, is learning—and centers and agendas are vehicles for learning on an ongoing basis.

WHAT IS AND ISN'T DIFFERENTIATION?

Let's start by examining differentiation and what the word means. Differentiation is more than different, and it is more than offering a choice of learning experiences to students. Effective differentiation is intentional. Teachers who are effective at differentiating match learning opportunities to students' levels of readiness, interests, and/or learning preferences. The teacher gathers information about what the students know about a particular topic or concept, their interests in the topic, and their learning preferences. In the capacity as instructional leader in the classroom, the teacher is the one who provides appropriate choices of learning experiences that will ensure challenge for individual students. Differentiation is for all students. The goal of differentiating is for each student to learn at an appropriately challenging level on an ongoing basis. After all, isn't that the purpose of school—for each child to learn?

When recognizing a concept such as differentiation, it is important to know what it is and also what it is not. Differentiation certainly implies different learning experiences, but they are different with a purpose. It is not different purely for the sake of being different. The purpose is to match learning experiences to individual students or to clusters of students to engage them in learning at appropriately challenging levels. Likewise, differentiation is characterized by different work, not by more work for certain students. It is not doing the assignments the class does and then doing extra assignments. Differentiation involves every child learning what he needs to learn in order to make appropriate continuous progress. Differentiation is grounded in the belief that all children of the same age are not ready to learn the same content in the same way and on the same time schedule. The authors also believe that fairness for students comes from the opportunity to learn what they are ready to learn, even if they are ready for more advanced content and can learn at a more rapid pace than their age-mates. That is how the one-room school operated when it worked well, and that is how a differentiated classroom orchestrates learning to address student readiness, interests, and learning profiles.

Centers are best known in primary classrooms, but they are equally useable and effective in classrooms of all grade levels. Teachers should not feel limited because they have not previously been in a situation in which centers are used at upper elementary or middle-level classrooms. Instead, they need to give them a try. No doubt, centers provide a vehicle for differentiating at all levels from kindergarten through middle school.

Centers make it possible to facilitate learning with students engaged in a variety of learning experiences. Therefore, in the classroom discussion that takes place after students have worked in centers, everyone talks about the same topic or concept; however, they share ideas and information from their learning acquired in a variety of learning experiences. That is a win-win situation for all learners and for the teacher—all students are engaged in learning with different resources and perhaps are working on a variety of products, yet they are all preparing for a discussion that they can have together. Everyone learns from what each student has learned, but each student has had the opportunity to learn what he is ready to learn. Therefore, the whole is bigger than each part.

DIVERSE LEARNERS NEED DIFFERENTIATION ON AN ONGOING BASIS

Learners differ in terms of their readiness to learn a particular topic, their interest (or noninterest) in that topic, and in their learning preferences (how they most like to learn). Learners also differ in the experiences they bring to the study of a specific topic as well as in their skill levels in critical thinking, creative thinking, research, problem solving, and decision making. These learner differences call for learning opportunities that facilitate and encourage learning at high levels.

Why Differentiate?

Why worry about children who are gifted and talented? Won't gifted kids be fine, and aren't teachers justified in spending most of their time and effort on children who are achieving below the level of proficiency or grade-level learning? Actually, the goal of schooling comes into play here: All children go to school to learn what they are ready to learn. Siegle (2008) stated in the Gifted Children's Bill of Rights that gifted children have the right "to learn something new every day." (See Figure 1.1.) Differentiating—so all children, including those who are gifted and talented, can learn on a continuous basis—is the right thing to do.

The quick answer to why teachers should differentiate learning experiences is to ensure that each child learns on an ongoing basis. How could anyone—parent or teacher—not advocate and plan for all children to be learning every day they are in school? For a long time, teachers have been expected to differentiate assignments for children who need more time and more basic information to learn. Differentiating for all students extends that planning to ensure academic success for all students, including those who need a shorter time and more complex content in order to learn on a daily basis. Differentiated learning experiences engage students in learning. Differentiation strategies allow teachers to tailor learning experiences to students as they manipulate the content from basic to complex, alternate the process from knowing to creating, and offer choice of products to demonstrate what has been learned. The teacher is the one in charge and, consequently, is the one who can make learning appropriately challenging for all students in the class.

REFERENCES

Siegle, D. (2008). *Gifted children's bill of rights.* Retrieved from http://www.nagc.org/uploadedFiles/PHP/Bill%20of%20Rights.pdf

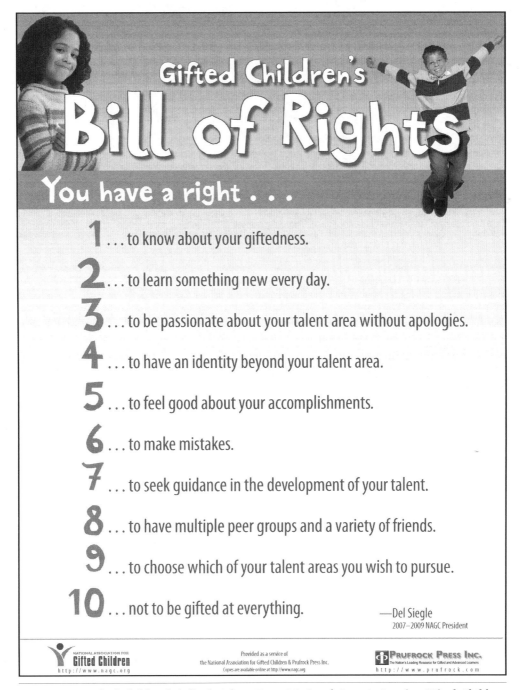

Figure 1.1. Gifted children's bill of rights. From National Association for Gifted Children (http://www.nagc.org). Reprinted with permission.

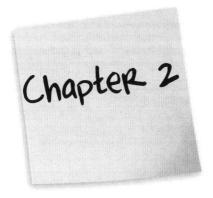

Chapter 2

Strategies to Use When Differentiating Through Centers

Julia Link Roberts and Julia Roberts Boggess

*When teachers differentiate, students who have gifts and talents
are more likely to show themselves and be recognized.*

—Susan K. Johnsen

Effective teachers make certain that all children and young people learn no matter how different they are. They translate differences into assets and allow students to soar. They remove the learning ceiling for all children, allowing them to learn what they are ready to learn. Ensuring that all students learn depends upon the teacher providing differentiated learning experiences. That statement holds true for a class of gifted children just as it does for other groupings of students, as children who are gifted and talented also approach a new unit of study with varying levels of readiness, a range of interests in the topic or concept, and different learning profiles.

SETTING THE STAGE FOR DIFFERENTIATION

Starting to differentiate at the beginning of the year is optimal. Starting early allows students to know that all children will not be doing identical assignments at that time or throughout the school year. Differentiating early on establishes the expectation that children will engage in a variety of learning experiences. In fact, parents and students must understand that it would be inappropriate, even wrong, for all students to be treated as one identical group. It makes no more sense to teach all children in a class with one set of lessons than it would for a pediatrician to prescribe one medication for all 11-year-olds just because they are that specific age—11 years old. That would seem foolish, and one assignment for all sixth graders makes no more sense.

Setting the stage for a differentiated classroom involves establishing the importance of certain principles. Roberts and Inman (2009b) describe three principles that create the appropriate climate for a differentiated classroom:

1. A differentiated classroom respects diversity.
2. A differentiated classroom maintains high expectations.
3. A differentiated classroom generates openness.

DIFFERENTIATION AS THE MASTER PLAN FOR LEARNING

Teachers need a master plan for a unit of study as well as for learning throughout a school year. Three basic questions direct the teacher's planning when differentiating learning experiences (Roberts & Inman, 2009b):

1. Planning question—What do I want students to know, understand, and be able to do?
2. Preassessing question—Who already knows, understands, and/or can use the content or demonstrate the skill?
3. Differentiation question—What can I do for him, her, or them so they can make continuous progress and extend their learning? (p. 9)

Question 3 comes into play only when students demonstrate that they already know most of the content at the level proposed and can demonstrate the skills. The important point to remember is that teachers can and do routinely differentiate by making assignments less complex and altering the pace for children who are working to reach proficiency. It is also possible and necessary to make learning more complex and to alter the pace for children who learn at a more rapid rate or who are at the proficiency level or beyond. Differentiating is appropriate across the spectrum of readiness levels with any content or concept.

ESTABLISHING THE STARTING POINTS: PREASSESSMENT

Preassessment provides valuable information to guide the teacher's decisions about learning experiences for individual students who then may be clustered for their assignments when it is found to be appropriate. The goal of preassessment is to discover what students already know so the learning can extend rather than repeat what they have learned. Julian Stanley (2000) entitled his article "Helping Students Learn Only What They Don't Already Know," a title that sums up the goal of preassessing students' knowledge and skills. When the teacher knows what children already know, she saves time and can use that time for extending learning for the child or the cluster of children who are ready to move on, continuing to learn about the same topic but at a more complex level.

Effective differentiation is characterized by students engaging in the study of a topic or concept in a variety of learning experiences matched to readiness, interests, and/or learning preferences. Differentiation is defensible when the starting point is established by information gained from the preassessment.

There is no one right way to preassess all of the time, but rather the preassessment tool must be selected by the teacher based on the information he wants or needs to glean from students—what information would help match learning experiences to where the students are ready to start with the content and skills, what are their interests in relation to the specific topic or concept, and what are their preferred ways of learning. By no means should the student always learn in a preferred way, but occasionally all children should have opportunities to do so.

Preassessment may be as simple as giving students 5 minutes to write about the topic or concept to be studied. If the content to be learned is sequential, the end-of-the-previous-unit assessment could provide the information needed to match learning experiences to the learners. Another possibility would be to give the students the opportunity to complete a T-W-H Chart (Roberts & Boggess, 2011; see Figure 2.1). In the T column, students tell the teacher what they are *thinking* about the topic, the W column lets them tell what they *want* to learn about the topic, and the H column gives them a place to say *how* they would like to learn about the concept. There are numerous preassessment possibilities. The teacher strategically can plan what will yield the information needed to facilitate high-level learning for all students in the class. Teachers must remember that high-level learning does not mean the same level of learning for all students, as that would not allow all students to continue learning because they are not identical in their readiness, interests in the topic, or learning preferences. Indeed, rigor is a relative term. A level of rigor varies considerably for a class of fifth graders and even for a class of children who have been grouped by readiness or ability.

Contrary to what teachers may think, preassessing actually saves time, that precious commodity that teachers find there is never enough of to let them teach everything that they want to teach. Consequently, preassessing needs to be something that teachers embrace and do regularly. When the teacher discovers that some children already know and can do what the unit has established as objectives, then those students can study the same topic or concept but at a more complex level. They can advance in their study of the content, and all students will be ready to engage in the discussion or in sharing products that add to the entire class' understanding of the topic or concept that is the focus of the study.

T – W – H CHART

Topic/Unit _____   Name _____

What do you **T**hink about this topic?	What do you **W**ant to learn about this topic?	**H**ow do you want to learn about this topic?

Figure 2.1. T-W-H chart. From *Teacher's Survival Guide: Gifted Education* (p. 91), by J. L. Roberts and J. Roberts Boggess, 2011, Waco, TX: Prufrock Press. Copyright 2011 Prufrock Press. Reprinted with permission.

FORMATIVE ASSESSMENT

"In truth, the teacher's job should resemble that of a water-skiing boat driver, and that job is two-fold: to drive the boat *and to check the skiers*" (Doubet, 2011, p. 10). This analogy of the teacher with the dual responsibilities of the boat driver is right on target with what the teacher's responsibilities are for all children's learning. The teacher is the one in charge, but she will only be effective if she checks on the learning as she drives the instruction.

Formative and summative assessments take different perspectives on learning. The former addresses whether learning is on track to meet the objectives, while summative assessment looks at what has been learned at the conclusion of the unit. Stiggins and Chappuis (2012) described formative assessment as assessment *for* learning rather than the assessment of learning. Formative assessment occurs throughout the teaching of the unit to signal the teacher when misunderstandings need to be corrected and when individuals or clusters of students need assistance to reach the learning goals and objectives. Formative assessment also lets the teacher know when a student or cluster of students is ready to advance to more complex content related to the unit of study or to have skills added to the expectations as other skills have been mastered.

Formative assessments come in many formats. The teacher may have students write about what they have learned that day and give it to the teacher as they leave the room, so the teacher can know what students understood and retained. Likewise, the teacher may have the students answer a question as class starts in order to check for understanding. This beginning-of-class formative assessment can be the "bell ringer" activity that students expect as soon as class begins. Teachers may also do learning-checks as they walk around the room as students are completing assignments. Using a clicker system is another way for the teacher to figure out what students know and understand as the unit progresses. The important point is for the teacher to check understanding throughout the unit and to do so with each student in the class, expecting each one to be learning on an ongoing basis and ensuring that no student is boxed in place with his learning (see Figure 2.2).

DIFFERENTIATING CONTENT, PROCESS, PRODUCT, AND ASSESSMENT

Differentiation can focus on the content, the process, the product, and/or the assessment. Teachers can differentiate one or more of these dimensions of learning experiences. Figure 2.3 shows how content plus process plus product equal a learning experience.

FIGURE 2.2. Don't box in learning. Lift the lid. Illustration by J. M. Bellemere.

Content

The content is what the teacher plans for students to learn. The content can be both basic and complex. Assignments can allow students to study the same topic or concept but at varying levels of complexity. Of course, the teacher is the one to decide the perfect match of content to students based on information gathered through the preassessment or what is known of their learning profiles.

Teachers add to the complexity of the content when they tie the major concept to a universal theme such as patterns, change, or structure. Most concepts can be taught at an elementary school level up to a college level. An array of resources opens up possibilities for all students to approach learning about the concept or topic at an appropriately challenging level.

Process

Process describes what students will do cognitively or the thinking that they are asked to do or perhaps are allowed to do. Basic thinking involves knowing and

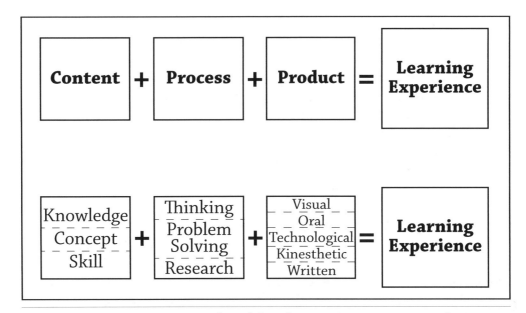

Figure 2.3. Learning experiences. Adapted from "Writing Units That Remove the Learning Ceiling," by J. L. Roberts and R. A. Roberts, in *Methods and Materials for Teaching the Gifted* (3rd ed., p. 199), by F. A. Karnes and S. M. Bean (Eds.), 2009, Waco, TX: Prufrock Press. Copyright 2009 by Prufrock Press. Adapted with permission.

understanding, while high-level thinking promotes creative and critical thinking. All children need to be productive thinkers, but not all children are ready to do so on the same time schedule and with all content areas. Once again, preassessment information informs the teacher as to what is the best match with specific students for the level of thinking (process) for specific learning experiences.

Twenty-first century skills place an emphasis on process skills—critical and creative thinking as well as problem solving and decision making. Wagner (2008) enumerated seven survival skills for the future:

1. critical thinking and problem solving,
2. collaboration across networks and leading by influence,
3. agility and adaptability,
4. initiative and entrepreneurialism,
5. effective oral and written communication,
6. accessing and analyzing information, and
7. curiosity and imagination.

These 21st-century survival skills include process skills and can all be incorporated in learning experiences in centers. Of course, these survival skills include a variety of skills, all of which are important for lifelong learners who will be productive members of society.

Darling-Hammond (2010) provided a different list of 21st-century skills needed by students to be successful as adults. These skills include the capacity to:

- Design, evaluate, and manage one's own work so that it continually improves
- Frame, investigate, and solve problems using a wide range of tools and resources
- Collaborate strategically with others
- Communicate effectively in many forms
- Find, analyze, and use information for many purposes
- Develop new products and ideas. (p. 2)

What do these lists of 21st-century skills have in common? That is an important question to consider, and the teacher's answer will focus on higher level thinking or process skills. These skills require far more than searching online for an answer or responding on a worksheet. Students need opportunities to engage in learning. These lists include research skills, communication skills, and thinking skills, but they also address the need for students to persevere—to accept a learning challenge or a problem-solving situation and to work their way through the problem. Learning in centers can provide the environment for developing and honing 21st-century skills.

Product

The product is the vehicle the student develops in order to complete a learning experience or assignment or to show what he has learned. See Table 2.1 for a listing of student products; this is not an all-inclusive list but a good one. Such products can be categorized in various ways. Roberts and Inman (2009a) used the following categories—kinesthetic, oral, technological, visual, and written. Karnes and Stephens (2009) delineated categories as visual, oral, performance, written, and multicategorical. Although these systems for categorizing products certainly are not the only ones, it is important for teachers to establish categories that organize the variety of products. For example, teachers may well think they offer a variety of products, but they actually are all written and traditional school products. Children with various learning preferences will often choose products that allow them to use their strengths if given the choice. Although students should not always work in their strength areas or preferred ways of learning, teachers should plan for all children to at least occasionally have opportunities to shine as they produce their projects. Students need to have opportunities that allow them to capitalize on their areas of strength, as that is certainly a motivator for many students.

The DAP (Developing and Assessing Products) Tool (Roberts & Inman, 2009a) is a protocol that guides students in developing products and aids teachers in assessing those products. The DAP Tool has four components that are the key elements for students to focus on as they develop any product. The first component is always the content. The content is usually the reason that the teacher makes any assignment.

Table 2.1
List of Possible Products

Advertisement (print)
Advertisement (radio)
Advertisement (television)
Application
Article
Audiotape
Biography
Blog
Blueprint
Book
Book Cover
Brochure
Bulletin Board
Cartoon
Case Study
Chart
Choral Reading
Collage
Collection
Column
Commercial
Computer Graphic
Computer Program
Costume
Creative Writing
Dance
Debate
Demonstration
Diagram
Dialogue
Diary
Diorama
Display
Document-Based Question
Documentary
Dramatic Presentation
Drawing
Editorial
Essay
Exhibit/Display
Experiment
Evaluation Form

Feature Article
Film
Game
Graph
Graphic Organizer
Greeting Card
Illustrated Story
Illustration
Interview (live)
Interview (recorded)
Interview (written)
Invention
Journal
Lesson
Letter (business)
Letter (friendly)
Letter to Editor
Mask
Matrix
Mathematical Formula
Mentorship
Mime
Mock Court
Mock Trial (attorney)
Mock Trial (defendant)
Mock Trial (judge)
Mock Trial (plaintiff)
Model
Monologue
Movie
Mural
Museum
Museum Exhibit
Musical
Newscast
Newsletter
Newspaper Story
Open Response
Oral History
Oral Report
Outline
Painting
Peer Evaluation
Pamphlet

Photo
Photo Essay
Picture
Plan
Play
Podcast
Poem
Political Cartoon
Poster
PowerPoint
Presentation
Project
Public Service Announcement (radio)
Public Service Announcement (television)
Puppet
Puppet Show
Questionnaire
Research Report
Review
Science Fair Project
Sculpture
Scrapbook
Script
Service Learning Project
Simulation
Skit
Song
Speech (oral)
Speech (written)
Story
Story Telling
Survey
Technical Report
Technical Writing
Timeline
Transparency
Venn Diagram
Video
Video Game
Volunteer Activity
Webpage
Wiki
Written Report

Products List

Dr. Julia Roberts and Ms. Tracy Inman,
The Center for Gifted Studies,
Western Kentucky University
gifted@wku.edu

Accuracy and organization of the content are very important for students as they plan any product. The second component of the DAP Tool is the presentation, and this component is the only one that changes from one product from another. After all, the features of a model differ from those for a monologue as they do from a graph or technical writing. The third component of the DAP Tool is creativity. To encourage creativity, these questions are posed: "Is the content seen in a new way?" and "Is the presentation done in a new way?" The fourth component is reflection. Reflection is important in facilitating ongoing learning and helping students connect one learning experience to another. It is critical to get students to see that each learning experience is a building block to future learning and not one to be dismissed as soon as the project is turned in.

Products offer numerous advantages (Roberts & Inman, 2009a):

- Products are engaging.
- Products are motivating.
- Products have "real-world" connections.
- Well-developed products require high-level thinking and problem-solving skills.
- Products provide a practical way for teachers to match learning experiences to students' preferred ways of learning.
- Products allow for and encourage self-expression and creativity.
- Products foster pride in one's work. (pp. 2–3)

There are so many reasons to allow students to engage in learning via products. In a time in which many teachers are encouraged to have project-based learning, centers offer a way to do just that.

Assessment

A fourth way to differentiate is through assessment. Different assignments need assessments to match the complexity of the task. One way to differentiate the assessment of products is to use more than one rubric. Rubrics guide students in completing the assignment at a level at which they want to perform and are expected to perform. Chapter 7 provides examples of rubrics. Teachers save time when they design rubrics that can be used multiple times and in a variety of learning experiences—perhaps in various learning centers over the course of the school year.

The DAP Tool (Roberts & Inman, 2009a) is a protocol that can be used by students to develop a product and by teachers as they assess the product. The DAP Tool has three tiers or levels of sophistication for each product. Therefore, different students in one class can be using different tiers of the DAP Tool to guide their work on a specific product. Once again, the tier the teacher assigns to specific students should be matched to student information gathered from preassessments or from the learning profiles. What experience has the student had with producing that specific product? For example, has the student conducted interviews previously? Has the student used the computer to design graphics? Figures 2.4 and 2.5 provide examples of DAP Tools.

One clear way to get teachers to differentiate with centers is to have the rubrics or DAP Tools ready to use. Making it simple is helpful for the teacher. Without a protocol, the teacher must design rubrics for each assignment and then for each product that is offered as a way for students to demonstrate what they know and are able to do for that assignment. When the teacher has to do lots of extra planning for differentiating, it is less likely to occur.

STRATEGIES FOR DIFFERENTIATING IN CENTERS

Numerous strategies can be used in learning centers. A few strategies are highlighted in this chapter and others are shared in the chapters describing strategies for various content areas.

Letting Centers Bloom

One way to organize differentiated learning experiences within a center is to use a cognitive taxonomy. The revised Bloom's taxonomy (Anderson & Krathwohl, 2001) is one way to do that. The taxonomy provides a guide for designing learning experiences at different levels of rigor in the thinking required to complete the learning experience. Rigor, of course, is a relative term, and teachers use preassessment data to plan appropriately challenging learning experiences for all students and to match the learning experiences to students based on readiness. The revised taxonomy changes the nouns from the original taxonomy to verbs, and it reverses the top two categories—evaluate and create. The new categories are noted in Figure 2.6.

Making learning experiences motivating to the learners is so important if the students are to engage in learning at high levels. Such learning experiences can prepare students to persevere, something that it is difficult, if not impossible to do, if the learning experience is not challenging.

Using the revised Bloom's taxonomy to design learning centers gives the teacher the opportunity to add depth and complexity of thought for students who are ready as demonstrated in the preassessment. A template for this planning form can be seen in Figure 2.7. An example of a completed form can be seen in Figure 2.8. Teachers will find this form helpful when planning, but they will share learning experiences with students in other ways.

One format for using Bloom's taxonomy in centers is to place the listing of learning experiences with instructions in a file folder. Colored folders are attractive, and laminating the folder preserves it so the center can be used another year. Figures 2.9 and 2.10 are examples of differentiated learning experiences, as they may be dis-

ESSAY Tier 1—DAP TOOL

CONTENT	▪ Is the content correct and complete?	0 1 2 3 4 5 6
	▪ Has the content been thought about in a way that goes beyond a surface understanding?	0 1 2 3 4 5 6
	▪ Is the content put together in such a way that people understand it?	0 1 2 3 4 5 6
PRESENTATION		
STRUCTURE	▪ Does the title link to the main idea? Is an effective attention-getting device used? Does it contain a well-worded thesis early in the paper? Is the essay organized into well-developed paragraphs? Is it logical in its organization? Do transitions lead from one section to another? Does each paragraph have one main idea? Does the essay come to a close and link back to the thesis?	0 1 2 3 4 5 6
ELABORATION AND SUPPORT	▪ Is there enough detail to support the ideas? Does all information relate to the thesis? Are ideas fully explained and supported? Is there a balance of general ideas with specific details? If quotes or other references are included, have they been used carefully and appropriately?	0 1 2 3 4 5 6
STYLE	▪ Is it written for the expected audience and purpose? Are appropriate words used? Are the sentences varied in structure? Is a suitable tone used? Is the author's voice clear? Is figurative language used in an effective way?	0 1 2 3 4 5 6
CORRECTNESS	▪ Is the essay free from usage, punctuation, capitalization, and spelling errors? If outside sources are used, are they cited correctly?	0 1 2 3 4 5 6
CREATIVITY	▪ Is the content seen in a new way?	0 1 2 3 4 5 6
	▪ Is the presentation done in a new way?	0 1 2 3 4 5 6
REFLECTION	▪ What did you learn about the content as you completed this product?	0 1 2 3 4 5 6
	▪ What did you learn about yourself as a learner by creating this product?	0 1 2 3 4 5 6

Comments

_____

_____

Meaning of Performance Scale:
6—PROFESSIONAL LEVEL: level expected from a professional in the content area
5—ADVANCED LEVEL: level exceeds expectations of the standard
4—PROFICIENT LEVEL: level expected for meeting the standard
3—PROGRESSING LEVEL: level demonstrates movement toward the standard
2—NOVICE LEVEL: level demonstrates initial awareness and knowledge of standard
1—NONPERFORMING LEVEL: level indicates no effort made to meet standard
0—NONPARTICIPATING LEVEL: level indicates nothing turned in

Figure 2.4. DAP Tool for essay, Tier 1. From *Assessing Differentiated Student Products* (p. 150), by J. L. Roberts and T. F. Inman, 2009, Waco, TX: Prufrock Press. Copyright 2009 Prufrock Press. Reprinted with permission.

MODEL Tier 1—DAP TOOL

CONTENT	▪ Is the content correct and complete?	0 1 2 3 4 5 6
	▪ Has the content been thought about in a way that goes beyond a surface understanding?	0 1 2 3 4 5 6
	▪ Is the content put together in such a way that people understand it?	0 1 2 3 4 5 6
PRESENTATION		
REPRESENTATION	▪ Does the model look like what it represents? Is it a clear representation?	0 1 2 3 4 5 6
CONSTRUCTION	▪ Does the construction make the model stable? Are the materials appropriate for the construction?	0 1 2 3 4 5 6
LABELS	▪ Are the labels clear?	0 1 2 3 4 5 6
CREATIVITY	▪ Is the content seen in a new way?	0 1 2 3 4 5 6
	▪ Is the presentation done in a new way?	0 1 2 3 4 5 6
REFLECTION	▪ What did you learn about the content as you completed this product?	0 1 2 3 4 5 6
	▪ What did you learn about yourself as a learner by creating this product?	0 1 2 3 4 5 6

Comments

_____

_____

Meaning of Performance Scale:
6—PROFESSIONAL LEVEL: level expected from a professional in the content area
5—ADVANCED LEVEL: level exceeds expectations of the standard
4—PROFICIENT LEVEL: level expected for meeting the standard
3—PROGRESSING LEVEL: level demonstrates movement toward the standard
2—NOVICE LEVEL: level demonstrates initial awareness and knowledge of standard
1—NONPERFORMING LEVEL: level indicates no effort made to meet standard
0—NONPARTICIPATING LEVEL: level indicates nothing turned in

Note. Adapted from *Strategies for Differentiating Instruction: Best Practices for the Classroom* (p. 208), by J. L. Roberts and T. F. Inman, 2007, Waco, TX: Prufrock Press. Copyright © 2007 by Prufrock Press. Adapted with permission.

Figure 2.5. DAP Tool for model, Tier 1. From *Assessing Differentiated Student Products* (p. 72), by J. L. Roberts and T. F. Inman, 2009, Waco, TX: Prufrock Press. Copyright 2009 Prufrock Press. Reprinted with permission.

played in a learning center. One set describes challenging learning experiences built around civil rights that would be offered to students who were new to this topic. The other set describes more challenging learning experiences for students who demonstrated that they already had some knowledge about civil rights. Both examples offer engaging learning experiences and choice. Teachers often can offer choice of products to students. In fact, anytime the teacher is more concerned with students learning the concept or skill rather than the specific product for demonstrating the learning,

Create (Formerly Synthesis)
This level requires the student to think about the content in a new or different way rather than to produce a creative product, as a creative product can be the end result of learning experiences at all levels of a cognitive taxonomy.
Evaluate (Formerly Evaluation)
This level requires the student to make a judgment and use criteria to support that decision.
Analyze (Formerly Analysis)
This level involves the student in breaking the material into parts and determining how the parts relate to each other.
Apply (Formerly Application)
This level gives the student the opportunity to show how to carry out or use a procedure in various situations.
Understand (Formerly Comprehension)
This level asks the student to demonstrate that he can construct meaning from the concept or topic being studied.
Remember (Formerly Knowledge)
This level requires the student to retrieve relevant knowledge about the topic or task at hand.
Teachers must ensure that students develop cognitive skills at all levels—top to bottom.

Figure 2.6. The six new cognitive process categories of the revised Bloom's taxonomy.

choice works well. Teachers will not give students a choice of any of the six learning opportunities but rather a choice of two of three learning experiences—therefore, the student has a choice but the teacher provided the specific choices based on preassessment data that indicated what students already knew about the topic. Products presented as choices should be equally engaging—not worksheets for lower levels and podcasts and skits at the higher levels. The goal is that all students are learning, and all students must be motivated to learn.

The caution when designing learning experiences based on the revised Bloom's taxonomy is to make the "create" category one that requires creative thinking about the content. Completing a creative product (drawing an illustration or writing a story) does not qualify as a learning experience at the create level, as a creative product can be linked with learning experiences at any level in the taxonomy.

	PROCESS	CONTENT	PRODUCT
CREATE			
EVALUATE			
ANALYZE			
APPLY			
UNDERSTAND			
REMEMBER			

Figure 2.7. Bloom chart template.

	PROCESS	CONTENT	PRODUCT
CREATE	Create	Fractions	Open Product/ Your Choice
	Create examples of an interesting, unusual way to use fractions or to teach someone else about fractions. Select a product to present your ideas.		
EVALUATE	Justify	Fractions	Persuasive Essay or Debate
	Justify learning about fractions in a persuasive essay or debate.		
ANALYZE	Compare	Fractions	Venn Diagram or Poster
	Compare fractions and decimals on a Venn diagram or poster.		
APPLY	Organize	Fractions	Number Line
	Organize fractions on a number line.		
UNDERSTAND	Explain	Fractions	Discussion or Role Play
	Explain fractions in a discussion or a role play.		
REMEMBER	Identify	Fractions	Chart or Pictures
	Indentify fractions on a chart or with pictures.		

Figure 2.8. Bloom chart: Fractions. From *Strategies for Differentiating Instruction: Best Practices for the Classroom* (2nd ed., p. 72), by J. L. Roberts and T. F. Inman, 2009, Waco, TX: Prufrock Press. Copyright 2009 Prufrock Press. Reprinted with permission.

- Select two civil rights guaranteed by the Constitution. Fully explain the rights in a series of illustrations with text, a dialogue, or a diary entry.
- In an essay, PowerPoint presentation, or illustration, develop two scenarios that illustrate one civil right and the issues surrounding it.
- Enumerate the civil rights guaranteed by the Constitution. Create a poster or skit.

Figure 2.9. Bloom chart tasks: Civil rights, challenging.

- Imagine a civil rights issue in the future. Write an essay describing the issue and its possible effects.
- In a PowerPoint presentation or debate, discuss whether the United States or South Africa (or a country of your choice) has more effectively dealt with civil rights issues. Carefully explain your reasoning.
- Select a civil right, then describe its impact on various groups that it protects. Present your findings in an illustration or podcast.

Figure 2.10. Bloom chart tasks: Civil rights, more challenging.

Differentiating With Think-Tac-Toes

The Think-Tac-Toe format (see Figure 2.11) provides a variety of learning experiences for young learners. The columns or rows are often labeled, and students are instructed to choose one learning experience in each row or column. For example, in a literature class the columns may be labeled plot, character, and setting, so each student chooses one learning experience for each of those three literary concepts. There is no intention of students trying to complete three learning experiences in a row (as in a game of tic-tac-toe), but rather to complete learning experiences they find both interesting and challenging while following the directions of the teacher.

The Think-Tac-Toe model for differentiated learning experiences can actually offer a pair of Think-Tac-Toe charts—one more challenging than the other. Once again, the teacher is the one who knows his students. The learning experiences can be designed to offer various learning preferences such as when teachers organize activities according to Gardner's (1983) multiple intelligences model. Consequently, the teacher uses preassessment data plus information about the student's learning profile to decide which version of the Think-Tac-Toe will provide the appropriate level of challenge. Time and preassessment prove to be the key to effective differentiation of content, process, product, and assessment.

Because rubrics or DAP Tools establish expectations, they must be available to guide students as they develop the products offered in the Think-Tac-Toe.

Differentiating With Sternberg's Triarchic Intelligence Model

Sternberg (1985) offered the Triarchic Intelligence model, which features three ways in which people can be intelligent—practical intelligence, creative intelligence,

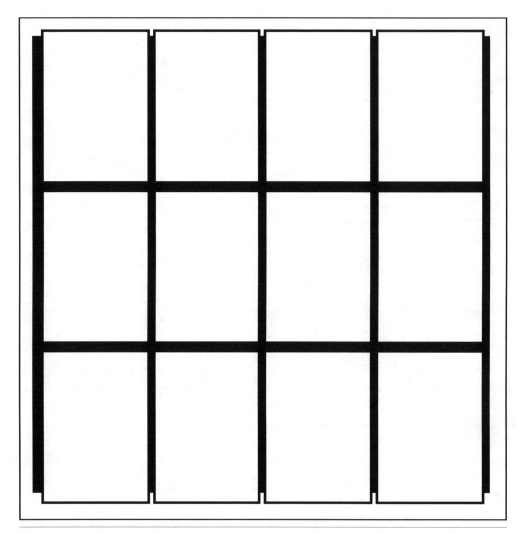

Figure 2.11. A Think-Tac-Toe template.

and analytical intelligence. Tomlinson (2011) described the three types of intelligences as practical intelligence being street smart, creative intelligence as imaginative problem solving, and analytical intelligence as school smart. These three types of intelligence provide approaches for differentiating learning experiences that can be used within centers. One approach may be more appealing to some students, thus creating student choice by allowing them to choose which assignment to complete within this model.

For example, a center with a focus on Sternberg's Triarchic Theory of Intelligence could have sustainability as the topic (it's one that could be studied at any grade level). This center would include various articles on sustainability. Students would be expected to make a 5–7 minute presentation after completing one of the three tasks in the center.

From the vantage point of practical intelligence, the assignment in the center could be to determine the three to five articles that were most interesting and practical to the student. Then the student would summarize the articles, highlight what the articles have in common, and make two suggestions that seem likely to work in order to advance or initiate work in the community (the community could be the classroom or school as well as the larger community).

From the vantage point of creative intelligence, the assignment in the center could ask the student to read three to five articles about the topic of sustainability. Then the student would be asked to imagine an ideal plan for sustainability in the community and describe it in detail. Illustrations could be included for a presentation.

From the vantage point of analytical intelligence, the assignment also would be to read three to five articles about the topic of sustainability. Then the student would select two or three of the most immediate problems that involve the theme of sustainability and provide solutions for one of them. The student is asked to decide who needs to be involved to maximize the possibility of implementing a solution to the problem.

The three types of intelligence provide a useful way to think about learning tasks that provide challenge and motivation to various students in a classroom. Students would have choice of tasks at the center. In each of the three learning experiences, the student would be reading about sustainability, thinking about its challenges in today's society, and pondering sustainability and its effects on the future. All students can be equally engaged in any discussion of sustainability, and all will make presentations to the class.

WHAT FOLLOWS IN THE NEXT CHAPTERS

The following five chapters provide guidance for educators in the development and implementation of learning centers. The dual intent is to provide examples of differentiated learning centers and to demonstrate models for teachers to use as they develop their own learning centers and agendas in a variety of content areas. The chapter following those focused on centers in content areas examines instructional management strategies, and the final chapter provides suggestions for learning more about differentiation through centers.

REFERENCES

Anderson, L. W., & Krathwohl, D. R. (Eds.). (2001). *A taxonomy for learning, teaching, and assessing: A revision of Bloom's taxonomy of educational objectives* (Abridged ed.). New York, NY: Longman.

Darling-Hammond, L. (2010). *The flat world and education: How America's commitment to equity will determine our future.* New York, NY: Teachers College Press.

Doubet, K. J. (2011, February). Formative assessment: The guiding force behind differentiation. *Middle Ground,* 10–12.

Gardner, H. (1983). *Frames of mind: The theory of multiple intelligences.* New York, NY: Basic Books.

Karnes, F. A., & Stephens, K. R. (2009). *The ultimate guide for student product development & evaluation* (2nd ed.). Waco, TX: Prufrock Press.

Roberts, J. L., & Boggess, J. R. (2011). *Teacher's survival guide: Gifted education.* Waco, TX: Prufrock Press.

Roberts, J. L., & Inman, T. F. (2009a). *Assessing differentiated student products: A protocol for development and evaluation.* Waco, TX: Prufrock Press.

Roberts, J. L., & Inman, T. F. (2009b). *Strategies for differentiating instruction: Best practices for the classroom* (2nd ed.). Waco, TX: Prufrock Press.

Roberts, J. L., & Roberts, R. A. (2009). Writing units that remove the learning ceiling. In F. A. Karnes & S. M. Bean (Eds.), *Methods and materials for teaching the gifted* (pp. 187–220). Waco, TX: Prufrock Press.

Stanley, J. C. (2000). Helping students learn only what they don't already know. *Psychology, Public Policy, and Law, 6,* 216–222.

Sternberg, R. J. (1985). *Beyond IQ: A triarchic theory of intelligence.* New York, NY: Cambridge University Press.

Stiggins, R. J., & Chappuis, J. (2012). *An introduction to student-involved assessment for learning* (6th ed.). Boston, MA: Pearson.

Tomlinson, C. A. (2011, February). *Differentiating instruction: 6 guidelines & some tools.* Presentation for Wedge Visiting Professor Series, Western Kentucky University, Bowling Green, KY.

Wagner, T. (2008). *The global achievement gap: Why even our best schools don't teach the new survival skills our children need and what we can do about it.* New York, NY: Basic Books.

Language Arts: Differentiation Through Centers and Agendas

Tracy Ford Inman

> As the plants grow, Mrs. Spitzer watches them closely. She checks daily for weeds and pests. She knows that different plants need different things. And that each plant has its own shape. Some of the plants grow quickly, pushing upward, eager, impatient. Some grow more slowly, unfolding themselves bit by bit. Some plants sprout thin and tall. Some are bushy and wide-spreading. Some are bold, showy. They are brightly colored, saying "Look at me!" Some are silvery and quiet, the color of the earth. A few are wildflowers and will grow anywhere you put them. And some need gentle care, a special watching-over. (Pattou, 2001, pp. 13–19)

As Edith Pattou so delightfully expresses through metaphor in her book *Mrs. Spitzer's Garden*, children do indeed walk into your language arts classroom every fall very different from each other in so many ways. They come to you with varying interests, needs, and abilities. Some will be advanced readers, for example, while others may be right at grade level or below. It is your job to ensure that your garden is fertile, allowing each plant to thrive. Whether they are like wildflowers or need a special watching-over, your students learn better when their individual learning needs are met. Opportunities for differentiation abound in the language arts classroom, and matching content, process, or product to student interest, need, or ability creates a rich growing environment for all.

Of course, the content, process, and product of the language arts centers and agendas must be aligned to your state standards. Most states have adopted the Common Core State Standards (National Governors Association & Council of Chief State School Officers, 2010) for their language arts curricula. All of the centers and agendas in this chapter directly address one of the writing, reading literature, or language standards. Organized by differentiation of content, process, and product, each section contains three examples: one for grades K–2, one for grades 3–5, and one for grades 6–8. Because the K–12 writing, reading literature, and language standards build on themselves, each lesson could easily be modified for another grade level. A key point to remember is that differentiation is only defensible when you preassess. You must answer this question whenever you teach: "Why is this particular child learning this particular language arts material in this particular way?" All of those answers should be found on preassessments that ascertain interest, ability or readiness, or learning style.

CONTENT DIFFERENTIATION THROUGH CENTERS AND AGENDAS

Differentiation of language arts content comes in various forms, from curriculum compacting to independent study. The bottom line is that once a student proves that he has mastered most or all of the material through a preassessment, he deserves the opportunity to learn new concepts about that language arts content. You can add depth and complexity to the content or venture into tangential aspects of it. Perhaps the simplest way to provide differentiation of content is through student choice, which could also be viewed as differentiation via interest.

These writing centers and agendas are based on student interest. The examples open up many possibilities for student choice from selecting fiction to writing about the aspect of the Civil War that most interests them.

Book Recommendations Agenda (Grade 2)

Student interest is addressed in two ways using this menu agenda (see Figure 3.1). First, students select a fiction book of their choice at their appropriate level. Second, they select menu writing options that most interest them.

Standard Addressed: Writing Standard 2.1: Write opinion pieces in which they introduce the topic or book they are writing about, state an opinion, supply reasons that support the opinion, use linking words (e.g., because, and, also) to connect opinion and reasons, and provide a concluding statement or section.

Lesson Hook: Ask students, "Have you read a book that is so good that you think others need to read it? Have any of you read a book that you think others should not read?" Make sure students give specific reasons for enjoying or not enjoying the book.

BOOK RECOMMENDATION MENU

Appetizer: Pick One

What do you think about the book?

_____ 1. Write a **title** that expresses your opinion.

_____ 2. Create an **attention getter** that expresses your opinion.

Main Dish: Pick One

Why do you think this way about the book?

_____ 1. Complete a **T-chart** with five thoughts/feelings and 10 textual references to support your thoughts and feelings.

_____ 2. Complete a **bubble map** with five thoughts/feelings and 10 textual references to support your thoughts and feelings.

Side Dish: Pick Two

Can you prove your opinion?

_____ 1. Write five **sentences** proving your thoughts expressed in the main dish.

_____ 2. Find five **connecting words** (such as *because, and, also*) used in your sentences or paragraph that prove your thoughts expressed in the main dish.

_____ 3. Write a five-sentence **paragraph** proving your thoughts expressed in the main dish.

Dessert: Pick One

_____ 1. Write a pro-book conclusion in a complete **sentence**.

_____ 2. Write an anti-book conclusion in a complete **sentence**.

Figure 3.1. Book recommendation agenda.

Assignment: The goal of this assignment is for students to recommend or not recommend a fiction book of their choice. Students are to choose a fiction book at their appropriate reading level, then read it carefully. They should then select options from the menu to complete. The options will guide their writing. All writing is to be shared during the class's rendition of *Reading Rainbow*.

Civil War Research Centers (Grade 5)

Language arts naturally complements many other disciplines, especially social studies. For example, Writing Standard 5.7: "Conduct short research projects that use several sources to build knowledge through investigation of different aspects of a topic" blends beautifully with the National Center for History in the Schools' (1996) United States History Content Standards (see http://www.nchs.ucla.edu/Standards/us-history-content-standards). This interdisciplinary lesson, involving interest-based centers on certain aspects of the Civil War, weaves the writing standard focusing on research with various U.S. History standards. Working alone or with partners, all students will conduct short research projects on an aspect of the Civil War most interesting to them. Each center should contain multiple print resources (preferably both primary and secondary sources) and, ideally, access to the Internet. Of course, instructions and rubrics should be included.

Center 1: Slavery and Other Causes

Standard Addressed: U.S. History Content Standard 1A: Explain the causes of the Civil War and evaluate the importance of slavery as a principal cause of the conflict.

Assignment: Using at least four resources, outline three causes of the Civil War, providing evidence and support. Be sure to include and evaluate slavery as a main cause. Write a report explaining what you think the main cause of the Civil War is; be sure to support this position with evidence you found.

Center 2: Military Technology

Standard Addressed: U.S. History Content Standard 2A: Identify the innovations in military technology and explain their impact on humans, property, and the final outcome of the war.

Assignment: Using at least four resources, explain the innovations in military technology (e.g., guns, ammunition, cannons). Also explain how these changes affected people and the outcome of the war. Include explanations, descriptions, and illustrations in a children's book entitled *Civil War Military Technology: Innovations and Impact.*

Center 3: War Leaders

Standard Addressed: U.S. History Content Standard 2A: Identify the turning points of the war and evaluate how political, military, and diplomatic leadership affected the outcome of the conflict.

Assignment: Using at least four resources, create an illustrated timeline that identifies the turning points in the war. For each major entry, highlight the leader(s) involved, explaining the decisions they made and how those decisions affected the war.

Center 4: Emancipation Proclamation

Standard Addressed: U.S. History Content Standard 2A: Evaluate provisions of the Emancipation Proclamation, Lincoln's reasons for issuing it, and its significance.

Assignment: Research the Emancipation Proclamation, focusing on why it was written, what it contains in it, and how it was important. Using at least four sources, report your findings in a PowerPoint presentation.

Center 5: Women's Roles in the War

Standard Addressed: U.S. History Content Standard 2B: Compare women's home front and battlefront roles in the Union and the Confederacy.

Assignment: Using at least four sources, research the role of women during the war. Compare and contrast women's responsibilities on the home front and women's jobs on the battlefront using graphic organizers.

Phone Book Writing: What's in a Name? (Grade 8)

This writing agenda encourages much student choice—from how to prewrite to where to publish. Although all students will have the same writing prompt, the Think-Tac-Toe (see Figure 3.2) affords them the opportunity for self-expression and individual approach to the assignment.

Standard Addressed: Writing Standard 8.4: Produce clear and coherent writing in which the development, organization, and style are appropriate to task, purpose, and audience.

Assignment: Through the writing process, students will create a narrative, explanatory, or informative piece of writing exploring a person whose name they have chosen from a phone book. They will be able to individualize the assignment in each step of the writing process.

Phone Book Writing: What's in a Name?

We have read and discussed several written works in different genres that explore an individual person. It's now your turn to write. Skim through several phone books, jotting down names that interest you. Once you have decided on a name, you will write a fictional piece that explores that person—physically, emotionally, socially, etc. You will individualize the writing process by selecting one activity from each row below. Remember to incorporate important genre conventions.

Prewriting	Brainstorm characteristics, likes and dislikes, physical features, and life components (job, family, education, etc.) of your person.	Create a three-circle Venn labeling the three circles *physical characteristics*, *personality traits*, and *lifestyle* of your person.	Using a technique of your choice, prewrite for your piece. Be sure to address the physical, emotional, and social aspects of your person.	In a web, prewrite for your piece. Be sure to include the physical, emotional, and social aspects of your person.
Writing: *Task Audience Purpose*	Paying careful attention to the characteristics of the genre, compose a poem about your person. (explanatory)	Paying careful attention to the characteristics of the genre, compose a short story about your person. (narrative)	Paying careful attention to the characteristics of the genre, compose an essay about your person. (informative)	Paying careful attention to the characteristics of the genre, create an interview with your person including both questions and answers. (informative)
Revising/ Editing: *Development Organization Style*	Read and critique another student's work using the DAP Tool. Give specific suggestions to improve his or her writing.	Write questions you want answered about your work; team with another student to critique each other's work. Give specific suggestions to improve his or her writing.	Conference with the instructor for guidance and insight.	Find someone outside of class to use the DAP Tool on your piece. Be sure that person gives specific suggestions to improve the writing.
Publishing	Submit your piece to be printed in the school paper.	Read your piece aloud to the class.	Post your piece to the Internet.	Submit your piece to a contest or magazine.

Figure 3.2. Phone book writing: What's in a name?

Prior to distributing Phone Book Writing: What's in a Name? Think-Tac-Toe (Figure 3.2), share and discuss examples of writing that analyze, present, or explore a name. The Beatles' "Eleanor Rigby" and E. A. Robinson's "Richard Cory" are excellent for this purpose. Students have already been taught the components and characteristics of several genre types, so they should be able to discuss development, organization, and style of the genres as well as understand the roles that purpose and audience play in writing. Be sure to pass out the rubrics or DAP Tools (Roberts & Inman, 2009a) when making the assignment.

PROCESS DIFFERENTIATION THROUGH AGENDAS AND CENTERS

Differentiation based on readiness or ability in language arts meets the needs of all levels of learners, whether they are ready for on-level content, in need of remediation, or in need of enrichment. In fact, this type of differentiation is perhaps the most effective for advanced readers or children who are gifted and talented in language arts. Gifted children's educational needs differ from other children with regard to pace and complexity (Kaplan, 2007; Parke, 1992). These children thrive when challenged cognitively (Gavin, Casa, Adelson, Carroll, & Sheffield, 2009), yet too often they are overlooked in the regular classroom and are bored (Neihart, Reis, Robinson, & Moon, 2002). Centers or agendas designed to meet different readiness or ability levels are a simple, yet effective, way to meet the needs of all children in your language arts classroom, including those who are gifted and talented in that area. Everyone will study the same concept at the same time, yet some will process the information on higher levels than others. The following examples use Think-Tac-Toes, Bloom charts, and centers based on the revised Bloom's taxonomy (Anderson & Krathwohl, 2001). Remember, the key to meeting children's needs here is the match between preassessment and the level at which the child is ready to learn language, reading, or writing skills.

Reading Literature (Grade 1)

When using Think-Tac-Toes or menus as the agendas in your language arts classroom, you can't simply mix higher level thinking activities with lower level ones on the same agenda. You have no guarantee that the child will choose the best match for his or her ability. Two versions of the same agenda solve that problem. Children ready for more complexity, such as advanced readers, get to choose from one set of options, while children who need to process new concepts at more basic levels receive another. As far as the children are concerned, they have choices in how they learn.

Standard Addressed: Reading Literature Standard 1.3: Describe characters, settings, and major events in a short story, using key details.

Assignment: Students are to select one activity from each row to complete. Remember to distribute rubrics when the assignment is made. Students ready for extra challenge will receive the Think-Tac-Toe in Figure 3.3. Figure 3.4 is for students ready to process the short story with less complexity.

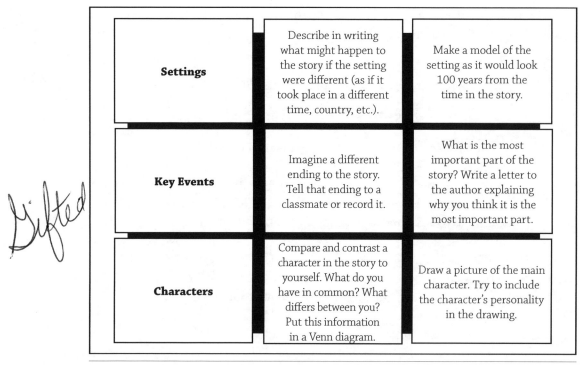

Gifted

Figure 3.3. Short story Think-Tac-Toe: Extra challenging.

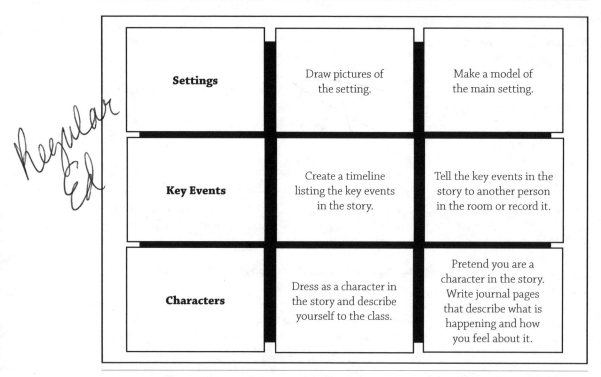

Regular Ed

Figure 3.4. Short story Think-Tac-Toe: Challenging.

Reading Literature (Grade 4)

This agenda is based on Bloom's taxonomy. Children will have a choice of three learning activities as they explore the differences in certain genres.

Standard Addressed: Reading Literature Standard 5: Explain major differences between poems, drama, and prose, and refer to the structural elements of poems (e.g., verse, rhythm, meter) and drama (e.g., casts of characters, settings, descriptions, dialogue, stage directions) when writing or speaking about a text.

Assignment: Students who are ready for more challenging reading or who think about literature at a higher level choose from selections on Figure 3.5 while students needing less challenge opt from choices on Figure 3.6.

The above ideas stem from the Bloom chart (see Figure 3.7; Roberts & Inman, 2009b) that is included here. Please note that students do not receive this chart; it is your planning tool.

Language (Grade 6)

These centers explore language and address the three aspects of the language standard: connotation and denotation, word relationships, and figures of speech. Because the activities address individual readiness levels in language skills, it is vital that students take a preassessment.

Standard Addressed: Language Standard 6.5: Demonstrate understanding of figurative language, word relationships, and nuances in word meanings.

Assignment: Based on the preassessment results, you will assign each student to a suit of playing cards (i.e., spades, diamonds, clubs). Students who have mastered the basic concepts and are ready to process the concept on the highest levels of Bloom select from those with a spade on them, students ready to process the concept in the middle levels of Bloom choose from activities with a diamond on them, and students who need to think about the concept on the lowest levels of Blooms opt for activities with clubs on them (see Figure 3.8). All children have choices—you have simply determined what their appropriate choices are based on the preassessment. Each child will select one of two options at each center. Plan for at least one day at each center.

Exploring Genre

Select one of the following three options to complete. Be sure to let the rubric guide the development of your product.

- Create a three-circle Venn diagram that compares and contrasts poetry, drama, and prose. Be sure to include structural elements (e.g., verse, rhythm, meter, casts of characters, settings, descriptions, dialogue, stage directions, etc.)
- A $100,000 literary award is being created to recognize the most outstanding type of literature. The donor must select one genre: poems, drama, or prose. Choose one genre and argue in a letter to the donor that it is the most worthy of the three for awards. Be sure to include structural elements in your reasoning.
- Select a poem, play, or prose piece from what we've studied this year. Predict what would happen to its literary value if it were rewritten in another genre. First, rewrite a portion of the piece into the new genre. Next, describe what impact the new genre would have on the literary value and popularity of the piece. Be sure to include structural elements in your discussion. Choose a product to present your ideas.

Figure 3.5. Genre: Extra challenging.

Exploring Genre

Select one of the following three options to complete. Be sure to let the rubric guide the development of your product.

- Using a graphic organizer of your choice, list the structural elements for poems, drama, and prose.
- Use an online collage/tag cloud generator (see http://www.tagxedo.com) to create a word collage/tag cloud for poetry, drama, and prose. Be sure to include structural elements (e.g., verse, rhythm, meter, casts of characters, settings, descriptions, dialogue, stage directions, etc.)
- Use an online tool to develop an avatar (http://www.xtranormal.com) that will explain the major differences between poems, drama, and prose. Be sure to include structural elements (e.g., verse, rhythm, meter, casts of characters, settings, descriptions, dialogue, stage directions, etc.).

Figure 3.6. Genre: Challenging.

PRODUCT DIFFERENTIATION THROUGH AGENDAS AND CENTERS

Many of you will find product differentiation easy to implement in your language arts classroom simply because so many product options exist. Naturally, as language arts teachers, we tend to lean toward written products such as essays, articles, or

	PROCESS	CONTENT	PRODUCT
CREATE	Predict	Poems, Drama, and Prose	Choice of Product
	Predict what would happen to its literary value if it were rewritten in another genre.		
EVALUATE	Justify	Poems, Drama, and Prose	Letter
	Choose one genre and argue in a letter to the donor that it is the most worthy of awards.		
ANALYZE	Compare/Contrast	Poems, Drama, and Prose	Three-Circle Venn Diagram
	Create a three-circle Venn diagram that compares and contrasts poetry, drama, and prose.		
APPLY	Classify	Poems, Drama, and Prose	Graphic Organizer
	Using a graphic organizer of your choice, list the structural elements for poetry, drama, and prose.		
UNDERSTAND	Explain	Poems, Drama, and Prose	Avatar
	Use an online tool to develop an avatar that will explain the major differences between poetry, drama, and prose.		
REMEMBER	Describe	Poems, Drama, and Prose	Word Collage/Tag Cloud
	Use an online collage/tag cloud generator to create a collage or tag cloud of poetry, drama, and prose.		

Figure 3.7. Bloom chart: Poems, drama, and prose.

Connotation and Denotation

 Using an online source that creates cartoons (such as http://www.gimp.org or http://pixia.en.softonic.com), design a cartoon that relies on connotation for meaning or humor.

 Create an imaginary interview with a poet of your choice. Predict what his or her responses would be to questions concerning word choice, connotation, and denotation. Use one or more of the poet's works in your questions and answers.

 Using an online source that blends words and photos (such as http://photopeach.com or http://animoto.com), develop a slideshow that illustrates both the denotation and connotations of words. Be sure to select photos that reflect appropriate emotions.

 Make a chart listing multiple words that, by definition, are the same yet differ greatly in connotation (e.g., ask, inquire, interrogate). Explain the varying meanings of the words.

 Make a poster that explains connotation and denotation for second graders. Include multiple examples of words, their definitions, and the emotions or images that are typically produced in the reader.

 In a graphic organizer of your choice, explain connotation and denotation using multiple examples.

Word Relationships

 Create an innovative way to teach word relationships or analogies. Write a lesson plan.

 The SAT used to include an analogies section. Write an opinion piece that argues for the reinstatement of this section of the test. Be sure to develop your reasoning.

 Select 20 words from a newspaper, magazine, or your English text. Incorporate those words into original analogies. Present them in a product of your choice.

 Go online to play two analogies games. Print your results. (Sample sites include http://a4esl.org/q/f/z/zz67fck.htm and http://www.quia.com/pop/14975.html.)

 Develop a game wherein players match the appropriate word to fill in the analogy. Be sure to use this format: [word 1] : [word 2] :: [word 3] : [word 4].

 Design a PowerPoint or Prezi (http://prezi.com) that describes relationships of words (e.g., cause/effect, part/whole, item/category) listing multiple examples for each.

Figure 3.8. Connotation, denotation, word relationships, and figures of speech.

Figures of Speech

 In a letter to the Common Core Standards board, argue why or why not figurative language should be included in the standards. Support your argument with passages from prose or literature.

 Using an online story creator (such as http://storybird.com), compose a short story incorporating original examples of figurative language. Complement the story with artwork.

 Find a poem or prose passage from the literature book containing multiple examples of figurative language. Rewrite the piece by taking away all of the figurative language and replacing it with plain language.

 Make a collage of figurative language examples that you have found in various print sources.

 Create a dictionary of figurative language. Include definitions and examples.

 Use an online tool to develop an avatar (http://www.xtranormal.com) that will explain figurative language through definitions and examples.

Figure 3.8. Continued.

---

poems. One reason for this is that writing is our comfort area—we know what makes a well-written essay, and we know how to assess a personal narrative. However, in order to meet students' interests, needs, or abilities, we must include all types of products: kinesthetic, oral, technological, written, or visual (Roberts & Inman, 2009a). The key to differentiating via products lies in assessment. Students must not only present accurate content, but they must do so in a worthy product that includes all of the necessary components. Before students can be held accountable for high-quality products, they must be taught what makes a particular product high quality and how to do that. Frankly, most teachers also need to be taught this as well. The DAP Tool (Roberts & Inman, 2009a) makes that possible.

The following three examples are based on three different approaches: learning styles based on Roberts and Inman (2009b), multiple intelligences as explored in Gardner's (1983) *Frames of Mind: The Theory of Multiple Intelligences*, and intelligences based on Sternberg's (1985) Triarchic Theory of Intelligence.

Language (Grade K)

Standard Addressed: Language Standard 2: Demonstrate command of the conventions of standard English capitalization, punctuation, and spelling when writing by capitalizing the first word in a sentence and the pronoun I and by recognizing and naming end punctuation.

Assignment: Based on a preassessment, you will assign each student a fruit: apple (analytical), pear (practical), or cherry (creative). Based on their fruit, students select one of the two tasks at each center (see Figure 3.9).

Language (Grade 3)

This Think-Tac-Toe agenda encourages students to select activities that best match their multiple intelligence (based on Howard Gardner's [1983] *Frames of Mind: The Theory of Multiple Intelligences*).

Standard Addressed: Language Standard 3.1: Demonstrate command of the conventions of standard English grammar and usage when writing or speaking by explaining the function of nouns, pronouns, verbs, adjectives, and adverbs in general.

Assignment: Explain to students that they will be able to demonstrate their learning in ways unique to their learning preferences by choosing a project option from the Think-Tac-Toe (see Figure 3.10). Be sure to pass out rubrics.

Reading Literature (Grade 7)

This agenda can be used in multiple ways—in small groups or individually, with an assigned short story or story of student choice.

Standard Addressed: Reading Literature Standard 7.3: Analyze how particular elements of a story or drama interact (e.g., how setting shapes the characters or plot).

Assignment: Because students naturally lean toward their learning style (e.g., kinesthetic, oral, technological, visual, written [Roberts & Inman, 2009b]), there is no need to list the learning style on the Think-Tac-Toe (see Figure 3.11). Ideally, students select one task from each category: plot elements, character, and setting. However, if time is short for student development of the product or your assessment of it, simply have students address one category. Or, you could be creative with the assessment and have students turn in their best product out of the three. Appropriate rubrics should be distributed when the assignment is given.

Capitalization

List the rules for capitalization studied so far. Write examples for each.

Rule: _____

Example: _____

Rule: _____

Example: _____

Explain why capitalization is important. Tell it to someone else at the center.

Capitalization is important because . . .

Draw a picture that shows what might happen if all capitalization disappeared.

End Punctuation: Period

On construction paper, make a mini-poster where you define the punctuation mark *period* and give examples.

Fix these sentences by putting periods where they belong. Use crayon.

I love to ride my bike My bike is green and has a bell I wrecked on my bike once and hurt my elbow My bike was not hurt though

Create a new symbol or shape for the period. Replace the period in these sentences with your new shape. Use crayon.

I help get dinner ready each night. I count out the forks, plates, and napkins and put them on the table. If the salt and pepper are not on the table, I put those on. Do you help get dinner ready at your house?

End Punctuation: Question Mark

Choose a book. Count the number of question marks and periods in the book. Write the numbers below.

Question Marks: _____
Periods: _____

How does a question mark look different from a period? On a separate sheet of paper, draw each and explain why it is important they do not look the same.

Make up a noise to replace the question mark. Make up another noise to replace the period. Read this passage aloud to someone else at the center using noises for punctuation marks.

I love apples. Do you like apples? Do you like bananas? I do not like bananas, pears, or grapes. No, that is not right. I love bananas in a banana split!

Figure 3.9. Capitalization, end punctuation: period, and end punctuation: question mark.

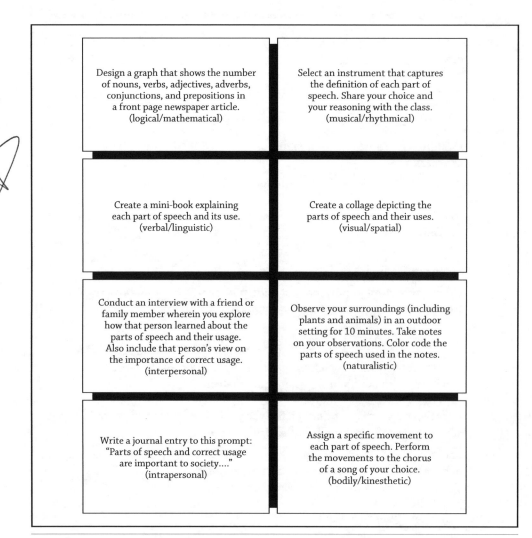

Figure 3.10. Parts of speech Think-Tac-Toe. From *Strategies for Differentiating Instruction: Best Practices for the Classroom* (2nd ed., p. 115), by J. L. Roberts and T. F. Inman, 2009, Waco, TX: Prufrock Press. Copyright 2009 Prufrock Press. Reprinted with permission.

PUTTING IT ALL TOGETHER: CONTENT, PROCESS, AND PRODUCT DIFFERENTIATION

Throughout this chapter, you have explored differentiation in language arts through content, process, or product. This last example blends the three in one simple agenda. Please note that differentiation in either content, process, or product helps meet the needs of language arts students through interests, abilities or readiness, and learning style. You certainly don't have to combine them, but there are certain concepts that readily lend themselves to it. A single preassessment (see Figure 3.12)

Plot Elements	Create a story map outlining the main plot elements.	Create cartoons highlighting the main plot elements.	Perform an alternate ending of the story in a skit.	Color code the main plot elements.
Character	Create a monologue showing how a character would react to a situation.	Illustrate what a character looks like based on the story. Incorporate personality traits when possible.	Compare and contrast a character in the story with someone in your life.	Write a blog of the main characters' thoughts.
Setting	Recreate the setting in a model.	Draw a series of sketches that illustrate the setting.	Describe in writing what might happen if the location were different.	Add or subtract 50 years from the time of the story. Develop a storyboard that explains the impact on the story.

Figure 3.11. Short story Think-Tac-Toe. From *Strategies for Differentiating Instruction: Best Practices for the Classroom* (2nd ed., p. 117), by J. L. Roberts and T. F. Inman, 2009, Waco, TX: Prufrock Press. Copyright 2009 Prufrock Press. Reprinted with permission.

combining multiple elements from the lesson gives you pertinent information to use when matching students to content, process, and product.

Differentiation of Content

Standard Addressed: Reading Literature Standard 5.2: Determine a theme of a story, drama, or poem from details in the text, including how characters in a story or drama respond to challenges or how the speaker in a poem reflects upon a topic; summarize the text. (Note, not only can this fifth-grade standard be taught through multiple differentiation strategies, but it also has variations in grades 1–8 that allow it to be altered easily to fit many other grade levels.)

Assignment: Students select a story or play of interest to them that is on their appropriate reading level (e.g., Lexile level, grade level). You may limit this to those options

---

Exploration of Theme Preassessment

Content:

1. What kind of literature do you enjoy reading? (This could be genre, subject matter, or author.)
2. Do you prefer to read stories or plays?

Process:

3. On the back of the paper, define theme. Then, explain a theme in one of the works you've read in the past year. Be sure to give examples from the work to support the theme.
4. On the back of the paper, summarize a fairy tale of your choice.

Product:

5. Circle those products that you have created before.
6. Put a star beside those products that interest you that you have not created before.

Diorama	Mask	Model	Sculpture
Debate	Interview	Monologue	Oral Presentation
Computer Graphic	Movie	Podcast	PowerPoint
Cartoon	Collage	Pamphlet	Poster
Diary	Essay	Letter	Written Interview

Figure 3.12. Preassessment.

---

available in their text or reader, or you may open it up to others. Your librarian could assist you with a list of choices.

Differentiation of Process

Standard Addressed: Reading Literature Standard 5.2: Determine a theme of a story, drama, or poem from details in the text, including how characters in a story or drama respond to challenges or how the speaker in a poem reflects upon a topic; summarize the text.

Assignment: Based on the preassessment, students receive one of two assignment sheets. Both have three options for students, but one focuses on Bloom's lower cognitive levels while the other incorporates the higher levels. Remember that all children need to think at high levels, but, for this particular lesson, the differentiation of process dictates that students have appropriately limited choices. Figure 3.13 is designed for students ready for extra challenge, and Figure 3.14 is designed for those for whom

---

Exploration of Theme

Each of you has selected a play or story on your reading level that interests you. Once the teacher has approved your choice, read the piece, keeping theme (i.e., the author's main message about life) in mind. There are two parts to this assignment: (1) a summary of the work, and (2) a project selected from the three options below.

Summary

Amazon.com has hired you to write a short summary of the piece you selected to be posted on its web page. In no more than 150 words, summarize the work in such a way that people will want to read it—they won't want to know the ending! In preparation, read several book blurbs from the website.

Project

Select a project from one of the three choices below. Be sure to get a rubric from the teacher once you have selected your product.

- Choose a piece of literature you have read in the last year that had a similar theme to the play or story you've selected to read for this assignment. Being sure to include the characters' responses to the challenges, compare the themes of the two works in a product of your choice.
- Place yourself into the work you've read. How would you have reacted to the events and other characters? What lessons would you have learned? How would you have responded to the challenges in the piece? In a product of your choice, predict your personal responses and reactions and describe the impact those would have on the theme.
- Determine two themes for the piece. Which of the two teach a greater life lesson? In a product of your choice, explore the two themes justifying the importance of one over the other. Be sure to include textual detail including the characters' responses to challenges.

Figure 3.13. Theme: Extra challenging.

---

less challenge is appropriate at this time. Please note that summarizing the piece is part of the standard, so the assignment sheets include a summary in addition to the exploration of theme.

Differentiation of Product

Standard Addressed: Reading Literature Standard 5.2: Determine a theme of a story, drama, or poem from details in the text, including how characters in a story or drama respond to challenges or how the speaker in a poem reflects upon a topic; summarize the text.

Assignment: Notice that all of the task choices in the agendas are open-ended. Students may select any product they wish to demonstrate their knowledge of theme.

Exploration of Theme

Each of you has selected a play or story on your reading level that interests you. Once the teacher has approved your choice, read the piece, keeping theme (i.e., the author's main message about life) in mind. There are two parts to this assignment: (1) a summary of the work, and (2) a project selected from the three options below.

Summary
A friend tells you that he is thinking about reading the work you just read. Without spoiling the ending for him, summarize it for him. You can e-mail him (write the summary as an e-mail and turn it in) or tell him about it (tape record what you would say or say it in person to the teacher). Be sure to keep it brief.

Project
Select a project from one of the three choices below. Be sure to get a rubric from the teacher once you have selected your product.
- Determine a main theme of the work you've read. In a product of your choice, collect sample passages from the piece that supports this theme. Be sure to include passages that show the characters' responses to the challenges they meet.
- Describe a theme of the work by focusing on one or two events that helped you understand the author's main message about life. Explain these events including how they relate to the theme in a product of your choice.
- How does the theme of the work relate to your life? Compare or contrast it to your life using specific information from the work and your life in a product of your choice.

Figure 3.14. Theme: Challenging

The two main considerations in their choosing would be that (1) they know how to create that particular product and (2) you know how to assess it. DAP Tools make this part easy (Roberts & Inman, 2009a). If you decide not to use DAP Tools, be sure to distribute rubrics before students begin their products. You may even want to limit their product options to ensure you have high-quality rubrics to accompany the products. The sample product list in Figure 3.15 incorporates multiple learning styles but limits the choices to those with DAP Tools.

As this lesson evidences, it is very possible to differentiate on multiple levels at the same time in your language arts classroom. But if this intimidates you, don't do it. Start simple.

FINAL THOUGHTS

Each differentiated language arts lesson you include throughout the school year helps make the soil fertile so that your garden thrives. Each time a child's needs,

Product List			
Kinesthetic Products:			
Diorama	Mask	Model	Sculpture
Oral Products:			
Debate	Interview	Monologue	Oral Presentation
Technological Products:			
Computer Graphic	Movie	Podcast	PowerPoint
Visual Products:			
Cartoon	Collage	Pamphlet	Poster
Written Products:			
Diary	Essay	Letter	Written Interview

Figure 3.15. Product list.

interests, or abilities are matched to content, process, or product in your classroom, the child blossoms. Pattou (2001) concludes *Mrs. Spitzer's Garden*, "And the year is over, and her job is done. But the plants will keep growing, uncurling their stems, stretching their leaves outward, and showing their faces to the sun" (pp. 25–26). Help your language arts students show their faces to the sun.

CHAPTER 3 RESOURCES

Analogies—http://a4esl.org/q/f/z/zz67fck.htm
Analogies (Set 1)—http://www.quia.com/pop/14975.html
Animoto—http://animoto.com
GIMP—http://www.gimp.org
PhotoPeach—http://photopeach.com
Pixia—http://pixia.en.softonic.com
Prezi—http://prezi.com
Storybird—http://storybird.com
Student Activity Center: Analogies—http://www.sadlier-oxford.com/phonics/
     analogies/analogiesx.htm
Xtranormal—http://www.xtranormal.com

REFERENCES

Anderson, L. W., & Krathwohl, D. R. (Eds.). (2001). *A taxonomy for learning, teaching, and assessing: A revision of Bloom's taxonomy of educational objectives* (Abridged ed.). New York, NY: Longman.

Gardner, H. (1983). *Frames of mind: The theory of multiple intelligences*. New York, NY: Basic Books.

Gavin, M. K., Casa, T. M., Adelson, J. L., Carroll, S. R., & Sheffield, L. J. (2009). The impact of advanced curriculum on the achievement of mathematically promising elementary students. *Gifted Child Quarterly, 53,* 188–202.

Kaplan, S. (2007). Differentiation by depth and complexity. In W. Conklin & S. Frei (Eds.), *Differentiating the curriculum for gifted learners* (pp. 79–88). Huntington Beach, CA: Shell Education.

National Center for History in the Schools. (1996). *United States history content standards for grades 5–12*. Retrieved from http://www.nchs.ucla.edu/Standards/us-history-content-standards

National Governors Association, & Council of Chief State School Officers. (2010). *Common core state standards: Key points of the English language arts standards*. Retrieved from http://www.corestandards.org/about-the-standards/key-points-in-english-language-arts

Neihart, M., Reis, S. M., Robinson, N. M., & Moon, S. M. (Eds.). (2002). *The social and emotional development of gifted children: What do we know?* Waco, TX: Prufrock Press.

Parke, B. N. (1992). *Challenging gifted students in the regular classroom*. Retrieved from http://www.nagc.org/index.aspx?id=143

Pattou, E. (2001). *Mrs. Spitzer's garden*. New York, NY: Harcourt.

Roberts, J. L., & Inman, T. F. (2009a). *Assessing differentiated student products: A protocol for development and evaluation*. Waco, TX: Prufrock Press.

Roberts, J. L., & Inman, T. F. (2009b). *Strategies for differentiating instruction: Best practices for the classroom* (2nd ed.). Waco, TX: Prufrock Press.

Sternberg, R. J. (1985). *Beyond IQ: A triarchic theory of intelligence*. New York, NY: Cambridge University Press.

Chapter 4

Using Learning Centers to Differentiate in Social Studies

Jana Kirchner

In the United States more than a century ago, the teacher in a one-room prairie schoolhouse faced a challenging task. She had to divide her time and energy between teaching young children who had never held a book and could not read or write and teaching older, more advanced students with little interest in what the younger ones were doing. Today's teachers still contend with the essential challenge of the one-room schoolhouse: how to reach out effectively to students who span the spectrum of learning readiness, personal interests, culturally shaped ways of seeing and speaking of the world, and experiences in that world.

—Carol Ann Tomlinson

Picture a typical classroom of elementary or middle school students studying social studies. They arrive each day often full of energy, with diverse reading abilities, and a variety of family backgrounds, interests, and experiences. In general, most of these students like to share their thoughts and what they know and, whether they admit it or not, most want to learn and hope that class will be fun! So how does a classroom teacher design social studies lessons to meet the diverse needs of this room full of students while targeting social studies standards? Although this may seem like a daunting task, the key is to create a classroom where differentiation is the norm.

Students are often overwhelmed with the many components of a social studies curriculum: names, dates, maps, events, places, primary sources, economics, and civics concepts . . . and the list goes on. Allowing students to interact with the content through learning centers or agendas is a way for students to make connections between the social studies disciplines and skills and to engage the content in hands-on, minds-on ways that target their readiness levels, interests, and learning styles.

GETTING STARTED WITH STANDARDS

The first step in creating a differentiated social studies class is to consult the national and state content standards for the subject and grade level. Although national content standards in social studies are in the planning stages at this time, each individual content area within social studies has specific content standards for grade levels. These national standards will be referenced for the examples in this chapter:

- National Center for History in the Schools (1996) standards: http://www.nchs.ucla.edu/Standards
- National Council for the Social Studies (2010) curriculum standards/themes: http://www.socialstudies.org/standards/strands
- Council for Economic Education (2010) economics standards: http://www.councilforeconed.org/ea/program.php?pid=19
- Center for Civic Education (2007) civics/government standards: http://www.civiced.org/index.php?page=stds

As a part of the unit or lesson development process, it is also important to consult the Common Core Standards (Common Core Standards Initiative, 2010) for Reading and Writing in History (see http://www.corestandards.org/assets/CCSSI_ELA%20Standards.pdf). These standards highlight the historical thinking, reading, and writing skills needed by students in social studies classrooms.

Of course, state and local standards are critical, as those often are the focus of end-of-year assessments for state and national accountability purposes. Those should guide the daily instruction in social studies classrooms.

After consulting standards, it is important to preassess students at the beginning of each unit. Preassessments can and should target interests, content readiness, and learning styles. The rest of the chapter includes specific social studies examples for grades K–8 based on differentiating for interests, readiness, and learning styles. All of these examples will work in a learning center environment where students work in certain locations throughout the room or as personal agendas where students work alone or in small groups. The last example will show how to integrate differentiation in content (interest), process (readiness/ability), and product (learning style) in one unit.

DIFFERENTIATION OF CONTENT
BASED ON STUDENT INTEREST

One way to differentiate for students in social studies is to vary the content based on student interest. Although all students are responsible for understanding key concepts or events, targeting students' interests will motivate them to engage social studies concepts with topics that pique their interest. The following examples show ways to differentiate content based on students' interests.

My Hero! (Grade 2)

Standard Addressed: Historical Thinking Skills Standard: Obtain historical data from a variety of sources.

Lesson Hook: Begin the class by having students answer the following questions orally or in writing: (1) What is a hero? (2) What kinds of people are heroes? (3) What traits do heroes possess? (4) Who is your hero? Teachers should guide this discussion and write ideas on the board. As a whole class, brainstorm a list of heroes they know from history. Share examples from Dennis Denenberg and Lorraine Roscoe's (2006) *50 American Heroes Every Kid Should Meet.*

Assignment: Students will choose someone who has been a hero in history. Once students choose their hero, then they will work in centers and research that particular person. Students can either complete this assignment individually at centers or in small groups. Figure 4.1 shows the assignment sheet that can be given to students. The teacher will need to provide library books, trade books, and a computer for students throughout the room. Students will research background information about their chosen hero, determine what characteristics or actions made him or her a hero, and choose their products to demonstrate their knowledge. Teachers should provide rubrics or DAP Tools to guide students' product development.

Packing My Suitcase . . . My Special Place (Grade 4)

Standard Addressed: Geography Standard 4: The physical and human characteristics of places.

Lesson Hook: If you could travel to any country in the world, where would it be? Have students prewrite to answer this question and share their answers and reasons with the class.

Assignment: Once students choose a country, they will work in centers focusing on that country. Students could either work in small groups or alone on this project. These centers need to have books and computers available for research. Using the detailed agenda task sheet in Figure 4.2, students will collect background information about their country. Once students have collected the information, they have to determine how and where the human and physical characteristics of places are

---

My Hero!

Your Task: Choose someone who has been a hero in history. Once you choose your hero, use the books, library resources, and the Internet to research information about your hero. Try to discover the following information:

- A picture of your hero
- Date of birth
- Accomplishments
- Adjectives to describe your hero
- Reasons for choosing your hero
- A good source to recommend if someone wanted to learn more about your hero

Your Product: Choose one of these products to create and share your information with the class. Include a picture and the information you learned above in your project.

- Design a poster of your hero that includes character traits of that person and reasons why you chose him or her as your hero.
- Write a letter to Dr. Dennis Denenberg and Ms. Lorraine Roscoe, authors of *50 American Heroes Every Kid Should Meet,* explaining why your hero should be included in their book.
- Write a rap that explains why your hero is important. Remember to create a catchy title!

Figure 4.1. Agenda for My Hero! center.

---

evident in their country. Students will create a travel brochure convincing tourists to visit their "special place."

"... And the War Came" (Grade 8)

Standard Addressed: National History Standards: Understand how the resources of the Union and Confederacy affected the course of the war; understand the social experience of the war on the battlefield and home front.

Lesson Hook: As a preassessment the day before the Civil War unit begins, have students participate in a gallery walk looking at Civil War images on each of these topics:

- role of women,
- battles,
- technology,
- prisons,
- medicine,
- a soldier's life, and
- military and political leaders.

Packing My Suitcase . . . My Special Place

Your Task: If you could travel to any country in the world, where would it be? Pick a country! Once you have chosen a country, you are to collect background information about that country. You may use books or online resources to research facts about your country.

Check the National Geographic Countries A–Z website for news and information about your country: http://travel.nationalgeographic.com/travel/countries. Find the following information:

- A map of your country, including the continent
- Type of economy with examples of goods produced there
- Climate and physical characteristics (such as mountains and rivers)
- Population
- Languages
- Religions
- A current event happening in your country
- Pictures of people or places located there

Your Product: Create a pamphlet or digital travel brochure that will persuade visitors to travel to your country. Your brochure must include physical and human characteristics of your special place.

Figure 4.2. Agenda for Packing My Suitcase . . . My Special Place center.

Locate period images from any Civil War digital collection website on these seven topics; place the images on posters around the room with a blank poster paper beside them. Have students spend 2–3 minutes at each station quietly recording their observations and questions about the images on the paper. Once they have rotated through all stations, have them choose a topic that interests them and explain their choice on an exit slip. The teacher can then organize research teams based on students' first or second interest choices.

Assignment: At the beginning of the next lesson, give students their chosen topic assignment. Have them return to that collection of images and comments and circle the most interesting or important questions on the paper. They may also add their own if some other questions pique their interest. These questions will guide their research and presentations for the unit. They will work in teams to examine primary sources, secondary sources, and images of the period to create a hypothesis about their topic and answer the questions posed by their peers. For example, the group researching medicine might determine whether or not medical treatment was effective during the Civil War and why or why not. Require students to support their findings with evidence from both primary and secondary sources. Students could be allowed a choice of products to demonstrate their knowledge, and a DAP Tool could be used to assess that product (Roberts & Inman, 2009a).

DIFFERENTIATION OF PROCESS BASED ON ABILITY AND READINESS

One strategy for differentiating the process of learning based on ability or readiness is tiered assignments. Tiered assignments allow students to work toward a common understanding of the social studies content but with varying levels of depth and complexity. Allowing choice within the leveled assignments also encourages students to develop an ownership in their work and product.

Using Bloom's revised cognitive levels (Anderson & Krathwohl, 2001) is an easy way to create tiered assignments. Roberts and Inman (2009b) explained differentiation using Bloom's taxonomy as offering "a variety of learning experiences on the same topic or concept by varying the process (verb), content (basic or complex), and/or product choices" (p. 61). In a Bloom chart, the content is what you want students to know, the process is the cognitive complexity based on readiness of the student, and the product is how students will demonstrate their learning. The following examples demonstrate ways to differentiate process using a Bloom chart in a variety of social studies content areas.

Members of a Community (Grade 1)

Standard Addressed: National Council for Social Studies curriculum standard/theme: People, Places, and Environment.

Assignment: In the primary grade levels, one of the key concepts in social studies is community. Students can examine their own local community and the roles of various community members and helpers. The basic principles of the national history standards for grades K–4 state that "to bring history alive, an important part of children's historical studies should be centered in people—the history of families and of people, ordinary and extraordinary, who have lived in children's own community, state, nation, and the world" (National Center for History in the Schools, n.d.). This first-grade-level Bloom chart (see Figure 4.3) addresses various roles of members and workers in a community. For both the first- and fourth-grade examples (see p. 56 for fourth grade), before giving the tasks to students, teachers should separate the Bloom chart into handout strips to level the tasks. For example, dividing the chart into three sections would allow two choices of tasks for students at three different levels of cognitive complexity: remember/understand, apply/analyze, and evaluate/create.

	PROCESS	CONTENT	PRODUCT
CREATE	Invent	Helpers	Skit or Paragraph
	Think about a new community helper. What would that person do to help?		
EVALUATE	Judge	Helpers	Oral Presentation or Series of Illustrations
	Review the things that three community helpers do and decide which community helper is most important to your school. Explain your decision.		
ANALYZE	Compare	Helpers	Venn Diagram or Short Story
	Show the differences and similarities between two community helpers.		
APPLY	Show	Helpers	Collage or Skit
	Describe how your town's community helpers work together.		
UNDERSTAND	Describe	Helpers	Dictionary or Chart
	Describe the job that each community helper does in your town.		
REMEMBER	List	Helpers	Poster or Illustration
	List the community helpers in your town.		

Figure 4.3. Grade 1: Bloom chart—Helpers in the Community. Used with permission by Julia L. Roberts and Tracy Ford Inman, Western Kentucky University.

Our State's Culture (Grade 4)

Standard Addressed: National history standard: Demonstrate understanding of the ideas that were significant in the development of the state and that helped to forge its unique identity.

Assignment: After studying a unit on state culture, students could be given tasks from the Our State's Culture Bloom chart (see Figure 4.4). One way to differentiate for students would be to cut the chart in half. The lower three levels of Bloom tasks would be given to students who need to grasp basic levels of the concept, while those students that are ready for more task complexity could be given the top three levels of Bloom as tasks. Students would still have choice within those levels as to which product they wanted to create, perhaps completing two of the three learning experiences.

State and Federal Branches of Government (Grade 8)

Standard Addressed: National civics and government standard: How are national and state governments organized, and what do they do?

Assignment: Besides Bloom charts, another way to differentiate process for the readiness or ability of learners is by leveling Think-Tac-Toe assessments. While keeping the content topic the same for both levels, the teacher can vary the process by designing choices of assessments that target different Bloom's cognitive levels. This eighth-grade example on state and federal branches of government has two levels: more and less challenging (see Figures 4.5 and 4.6). Students would be given the task sheet with the same branches of government (the same content), but with different levels of task complexity as choices. Teachers can decide how many of the tasks students complete, or students could complete all three categories and choose their best work to turn in to the teacher.

DIFFERENTIATION OF PRODUCT BASED ON LEARNING STYLES AND MULTIPLE INTELLIGENCES

Product development may be one of the easiest ways to differentiate for students because a plethora of products abound. Products may be technological (e.g., blogs, web pages, PowerPoint presentations), visual (e.g., posters, pamphlets, drawings), written (e.g., essays, vignettes, articles), oral (e.g., speeches, interviews, monologues), or kinesthetic (e.g., models, dioramas, role-play; Roberts & Inman, 2009b). The most difficult aspect of this type of differentiation lies in the assessment of the product. Teachers must be sure to hold students accountable for all necessary compo-

	PROCESS	CONTENT	PRODUCT
CREATE	Create	Places of Interest	Poster or TV Ad
	Create a new place of interest for the state.		
EVALUATE	Justify	Places of Interest	Travel Brochure or Podcast
	Judge the cultural and economic impact of one place of interest in the state.		
ANALYZE	Research	Places of Interest	Newspaper Article or Travel Brochure
	Research a place of interest in the state and persuade others to visit.		
APPLY	Determine	Places of Interest	Map With Illustrations or PowerPoint
	Find the geographical locations of places of interest in the state. Create a map highlighting them.		
UNDERSTAND	Explain	Places of Interest	Photographic Essay or Illustration
	Explain why certain places are frequently visited by tourists.		
REMEMBER	Identify	Places of Interest	Class Chart
	Poll the class to identify places of interest around our community and in the state.		

Figure 4.4. Grade 4: Bloom chart—Places of Interest. Used with permission by Julia L. Roberts and Tracy Ford Inman, Western Kentucky University.

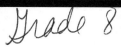

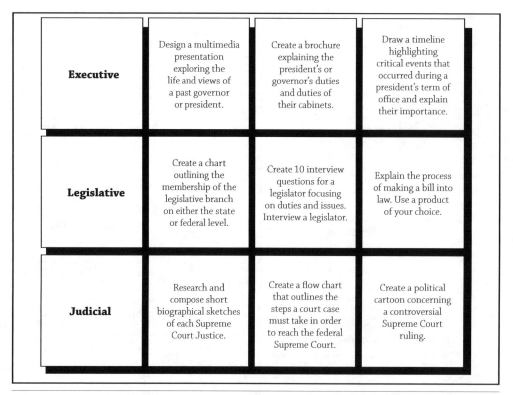

Executive	Design a multimedia presentation exploring the life and views of a past governor or president.	Create a brochure explaining the president's or governor's duties and duties of their cabinets.	Draw a timeline highlighting critical events that occurred during a president's term of office and explain their importance.
Legislative	Create a chart outlining the membership of the legislative branch on either the state or federal level.	Create 10 interview questions for a legislator focusing on duties and issues. Interview a legislator.	Explain the process of making a bill into law. Use a product of your choice.
Judicial	Research and compose short biographical sketches of each Supreme Court Justice.	Create a flow chart that outlines the steps a court case must take in order to reach the federal Supreme Court.	Create a political cartoon concerning a controversial Supreme Court ruling.

Figure 4.5. Federal and state branches of government, less challenging Think-Tac-Toe. From *Strategies for Differentiating Instruction: Best Practices for the Classroom* (2nd ed., p. 122), by J. L. Roberts and T. F. Inman, 2009, Waco, TX: Prufrock Press. Copyright 2009 Prufrock Press. Reprinted with permission.

nents of the product itself in addition to the content. Students must also be taught how to create high-quality products. That's one reason the DAP Tool is so effective (Roberts & Inman, 2009a).

The following three examples are based on two different approaches: learning styles based on Roberts and Inman (2009b) and multiple intelligences as explored in Gardner's (1983) *Frames of Mind: The Theory of Multiple Intelligences*. When creating these choices, make sure to include options for all types of intelligences and learning styles. Also, allowing students to develop a different product, even if it's not on the list, is a great way to let them have choice and ownership in demonstrating their content knowledge. In *The Ultimate Guide for Student Product Development and Evaluation* (2nd ed.), Karnes and Stephens (2009) included hundreds of ideas for student products with criteria for each one.

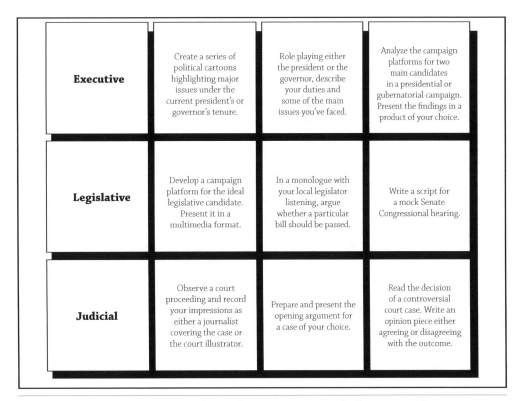

Executive	Create a series of political cartoons highlighting major issues under the current president's or governor's tenure.	Role playing either the president or the governor, describe your duties and some of the main issues you've faced.	Analyze the campaign platforms for two main candidates in a presidential or gubernatorial campaign. Present the findings in a product of your choice.
Legislative	Develop a campaign platform for the ideal legislative candidate. Present it in a multimedia format.	In a monologue with your local legislator listening, argue whether a particular bill should be passed.	Write a script for a mock Senate Congressional hearing.
Judicial	Observe a court proceeding and record your impressions as either a journalist covering the case or the court illustrator.	Prepare and present the opening argument for a case of your choice.	Read the decision of a controversial court case. Write an opinion piece either agreeing or disagreeing with the outcome.

Figure 4.6. Federal and state branches of government, more challenging Think-Tac-Toe. From *Strategies for Differentiating Instruction: Best Practices for the Classroom* (2nd ed., p. 123), by J. L. Roberts and T. F. Inman, 2009, Waco, TX: Prufrock Press. Copyright 2009 Prufrock Press. Reprinted with permission.

Think-Tac-Toe: America the Beautiful (Grade K–1)

Standard Addressed: National history standard: Demonstrate understanding of national symbols through which American values and principles are expressed.

Assignment: The following Think-Tac-Toe (see Figure 4.7) could be used as a final assessment for a unit on America. Students could be allowed to choose from two of the three categories (symbols, songs, and places) and work in learning centers or small groups with agendas. An "America Day," where all students could share their products would be a fun way to end this unit.

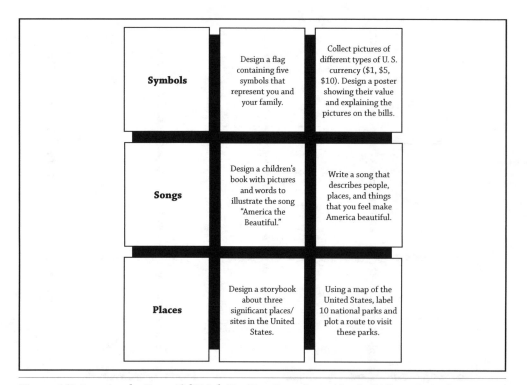

Figure 4.7. America the Beautiful Think-Tac-Toe. From *Strategies for Differentiating Instruction: Best Practices for the Classroom* (2nd ed., p. 106), by J. L. Roberts and T. F. Inman, 2009, Waco, TX: Prufrock Press. Copyright 2009 Prufrock Press. Reprinted with permission.

Lewis and Clark's Journey (Grade 5)

Standard Addressed: National history standard: Understand United States territorial expansion between 1801 and 1861 and how it affected relations with external powers and Native Americans.

Assignment: This menu of tasks (see Figure 4.8) is a final assessment for a lesson on Lewis and Clark's expedition. For the lesson, students examine excerpts from Lewis and Clark's journal entries, model artifacts, and maps of the journey to answer the following question: What impact did the environment and the Native Americans have on Lewis and Clark's journey? (Kirchner, Helm, Pierce, & Galloway, 2011). To explain their hypothesis, students will choose from a menu of products. The menu will consist of appetizers, main dishes, side dishes, and desserts; each of the tasks addresses a different learning style so that students can self-differentiate. Students will pick one appetizer, one main dish, two side dishes, and an optional dessert.

Appetizer: Pick One

_____ 1. Make trading cards for Lewis and Clark.

_____ 2. Write a song about the journey.

Main Dish: Pick One
What impact did the environment and Native Americans have on Lewis and Clark's journey? Answer in one of these products. You must include evidence!

_____ 1. Travel brochure

_____ 2. Photo story

_____ 3. Diorama

Side Dish: Pick Two

_____ 1. Write a journal entry from a Native American perspective.

_____ 2. Create a collage of three accomplishments of the Corps of Discovery.

_____ 3. Write a script of a conversation between Lewis and Clark.

_____ 4. Design a comic strip depicting a scene from the journey.

Dessert: (Optional)

_____ 1. Create a bumper sticker of Lewis and Clark's greatest accomplishment.

_____ 2. Design a Facebook page for Lewis or Clark.

Figure 4.8. Lewis and Clark's Journey menu. Adapted from "History + Mystery = Inquiring Young Historians: Experiences From a Teaching American History Grant" by J. Kirchner, A. Helm, K. Pierce, & M. Galloway, 2011, January/February, _Social Studies and the Young Learner_, pp. P3–P4. Copyright 2011 by National Council for the Social Studies. Adapted with permission.

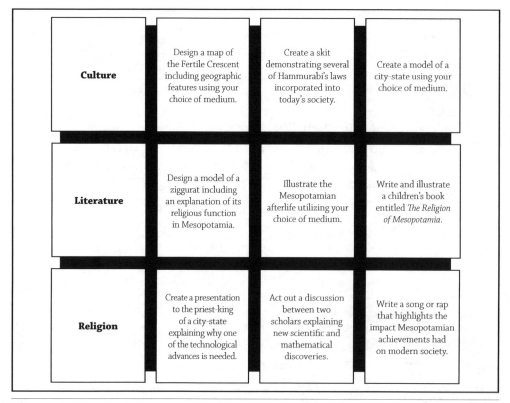

Figure 4.9. Mesopotamia Think-Tac-Toe. Adapted from *Strategies for Differentiating Instruction: Best Practices for the Classroom* (2nd ed., p. 104), by J. L. Roberts and T. F. Inman, 2009, Waco, TX: Prufrock Press. Copyright 2009 Prufrock Press. Adapted with permission.

Think-Tac-Toe: Mesopotamia (Grade 7)

Standard Addressed: National history standard: Understand how Mesopotamia became a center of dense population, urbanization, and cultural innovation in the fourth and third millennia BCE.

Assignment: This Think-Tac-Toe (see Figure 4.9) could be either a formative or summative assessment for a unit on Mesopotamia. Students could work in learning centers or with small-group agendas to choose a product from each category: culture, religion, and achievements. Students could choose the two best products to turn in to the teacher or display in the room.

Think-Tac-Toe Examples

In *Standards-Based Activities and Assessments for the Differentiated Classroom*, Coil (2004) gave multiple social studies examples of Think-Tac-Toes and tiered lessons that assessed a variety of student learning styles and ability levels. Her work included social studies examples from these content areas:

- U.S. History and Government—Civil War, early settlers, election campaigns, Native Americans, westward movement, World War II
- World History—Ancient Egypt, early explorations, math in history,
- Geography—Africa, Asia, Australia, Europe, five themes of geography, map skills, North America, oceans, landforms, South America, southeast Asia, rainforest
- Economics—Stock market

DIFFERENTIATING FOR CONTENT, PROCESS, AND PRODUCT? ALL IN ONE UNIT? IT'S POSSIBLE . . . AND EXCITING!

In *Differentiation Strategies for Social Studies*, Conklin (2004) described leveled learning centers as "the best of both worlds—choices and tiered assignments. Leveled learning centers are centers with activities that are leveled according to academic difficulty, but with choices of content and product" (p. 172). Using these leveled learning centers, Parker (2004) gave an example of how to create leveled assessment tasks incorporating student choice in a unit on immigration. The unit begins with excerpts of actual letters written by immigrants from China and Poland, coming to the U.S. through Angel Island and Ellis Island, respectively. For the assessment tasks, students may choose either the Angel Island or the Ellis Island experience. Students are then given a colored cube (green for above grade level; red for on grade level; blue for below grade level and English language learners) based on their readiness or ability level. Each cube has a different assessment task on each side (six total) that targets different learning styles, and students may choose from the six tasks. That's differentiating for interest, ability, and learning style. Wow! So let's see how it's done in a fifth-grade classroom studying a U.S. history unit entitled America Travels West.

America Travels West (Grade 5)

Standards Addressed: National History Standard: Understand the settlement of the West; Common Core Reading/Writing History Standard: Analyze multiple accounts of the same event or topic, noting important similarities and differences in the point of view they represent.

Lesson Background: Picture this scene. As the fifth-grade students enter the classroom, it is obvious that something exciting is going to happen. Today starts the westward expansion unit! With careful planning and a commitment to differentiation, the following unit can be designed to target the interests, abilities, and learning styles of a very diverse classroom of students through choices in content, process, and product. Of course, this unit can be modified for grades above and below fifth grade by altering the number of sources, complexity of the tasks, and levels of reading materials.

The first step in the lesson is creating an essential question (i.e., the "big idea") that students need to know and understand at the end of the unit. For this unit, the question is "Was westward expansion good for the United States?" Before starting the unit, the teacher would preassess the students using Figure 4.10 to determine their interest areas and background knowledge of the content.

Assignment: Students will participate in all aspects of the unit, taking on the persona of someone in their chosen group: Native American, railroad investor, or pioneer. Each phase of this lesson is differentiated. Phase 1 allows students to choose and research a group based on topic interest (content). Phase 2 allows differentiated learning experiences targeting ability or readiness (process). Phase 3 allows students to choose how to present their group's point of view toward westward expansion (product). Within their chosen groups, students could work in smaller groups of two or three. Students will spend approximately 1–2 class periods in each of these phases:

- Phase 1—Who are you? Why do you care about the U.S. expanding west?
- Phase 2—What happened during westward expansion in the U.S.?
- Phase 3—What does your group think about westward expansion? What evidence leads you to this conclusion?

Within each phase, there will be three centers (i.e., Native Americans, railroad investors, pioneers) around the room with materials and sources to help students research their group. Organizing materials and tasks ahead of time is critical for effective classroom management and smooth transitions between phases. At each phase, students will research information and add it to their westward expansion clue packet (see Figure 4.11) as an ongoing formative assessment for the unit. Throughout the unit, the teacher should show students sample DAP Tools or rubrics to guide their work on products (Roberts & Inman, 2009a).

Phase 1—Who are you? Why do you care about the U.S. expanding west? (Choices of content topics based on student interest). Students will choose one of the three groups and continue through all phases of the lesson thinking from that perspective: Native American, railroad investor, or a pioneer travelling west. The teacher would need to include group choice on the preassessment (see Figure 4.10) the day before the unit starts so students can begin working immediately at their center. One source for this center is Coan's (2007) *Leveled Texts for Social Studies: Expanding and Preserving the Union.*

Content: In the westward expansion unit, you will think like a historian, examine clues, and learn how different groups of people had different perspectives on events. Rank your preferences on which group you'd like to choose by numbering 1–3 (1=top choice; 3=last choice). Beside your top 2 choices, include a sentence explaining why this topic interests you.

_____ Native American

_____ Pioneer

_____ Railroad investor

Process: As we begin our journey through westward expansion, think about the books, movies, TV shows, or pictures you've seen about this time period. List what facts you know, your thoughts about the period, and questions you'd like to figure out. Use the back of the paper if you need more room.

I know that . . .	I think that . . .	I wonder about . . .

Product:
1. Circle those products that you have created before.
2. Put a star beside those products that interest you that you have not created before.

Diorama	Song	Model	Written Interview
Debate	Interview	Monologue	Oral Presentation
Computer Graphic	Movie	Podcast	PowerPoint
Cartoon	Collage	Pamphlet	Poster
Diary	Essay	Letter	

Figure 4.10. Preassessment for America Travels West!

This resource contains leveled texts on the Louisiana Purchase, the westward journey of Lewis and Clark, American Indians in the 1800s, pioneer trails, and Indian wars that would work as background information for all groups. Using various shapes on the bottom of texts to indicate reading levels from second to sixth grade, the book

You be the historian! As you move through all of the phases of this unit, you must carefully examine the "clues" and collect facts or evidence to help you understand your group and the events that happened during the age of westward expansion. In Phase 3, you will use all of the evidence to take a position on the essential question and present it to the class.

Phase 1: Who are you? _____
Include details about your particular group from the sources you used.
Where do you live, or where are you going?

What is happening where you live or on the trail?

Why do you care about westward expansion?

Summarize: Who are you?

Phase 2: What happened during westward expansion in the U.S.?

Evidence from maps:

Evidence from images and paintings:

Evidence from other primary sources:

Phase 3: What does your group think about westward expansion? What evidence leads you to this conclusion?

Figure 4.11. Clue packet: Was westward expansion good for the U.S.?

also includes a CD with the text and images used in the book. Images may be included at each center to supplement texts. Additional sources include:

- Any elementary-level U.S. history textbook (may use middle and high school U.S. history texts as well)
- Library of Congress Primary Source Sets: Westward Expansion—http://www.loc.gov/teachers/classroommaterials/primarysourcesets/westward
- Library books on the topics

Task. Students will research the background on their group with sources provided at their station. Use the following questions to guide the research:

- Where do you live, or where are you going?

- What is happening where you live or on the trail?
- Why do you care about westward expansion?
- What sources did you use for this information?

Phase 1 assessment. Students will collect information on their westward expansion clue packet (see Figure 4.11). Teachers may want to assess these before students move to Phase 2.

Phase 2: What happened during westward expansion in the U.S.? (Choices of process based on ability/readiness). As students move to Phase 2 of the lesson, they will continue in their chosen group and research important events that occurred during the era of westward expansion. These centers include three types of sources about westward expansion: maps, images and paintings, and other primary sources such as journals and railroad schedules. Each center has the same resources, but students will examine them from their group's point of view. For instance, all groups will view John Gast's *American Progress* painting, but they should examine its meaning from the point of view of a Native American, railroad investor, or pioneer. Teachers can either print images and maps for each station or include computers for students to access the websites.

Task. Students will examine the three types of sources located at their center. As a group, they will determine what the important facts are about events during westward expansion, and add them to their clue packet. Students should make sure to include their source for the content. Sources for Phase 2 centers include:

1. Maps and Chronology:
   a. U.S. Railroads 1826–1850—http://oldrailhistory.com
   b. Interactive Map: Westward Expansion—http://www.eduplace.com/kids/socsci/books/applications/imaps/maps/g5s_u5/index.html
   c. New Perspectives on the West—http://www.pbs.org/weta/thewest/events

2. Images/Paintings:
   a. John Gast's *American Progress* (with explanation on Picturing U.S. History site)—http://picturinghistory.gc.cuny.edu/item.php?item_id=180
   b. Edward S. Curtis's The North American Indian Photographic Images—http://memory.loc.gov/ammem/award98/ienhtml/curthome.html (The 19th-century images on this site are organized by U.S. geographic region and specific Indian tribe. Any of these images would work to include at the center.)
   c. Photographs of the American West: 1861–1912—http://www.archives.gov/research/american-west

   d.   Smithsonian American Art Museum's Lure of the West—http://
        americanart.si.edu/exhibitions/online/t2go/1lw

3.   Other Primary Sources:
   a.   Excerpts from Kate Dunlap's diary entries on her journey from Iowa to
        Montana by horse team, 1864—http://contentdm.lib.byu.edu/Diaries/
        image/4262.pdf (These diary entries describe the geography of the route,
        food and camping conditions, encounters with Indian tribes, and trouble
        with thieves. Dunlap's husband served as captain of the company, and
        Dunlap writes about her duties as cook and laundress for the company.)
   b.   Karen Baicker's (2002) *The Westward Movement*—This book contains
        numerous examples of primary sources that would work at centers. Some
        useful examples are a pioneer train constitution, journal excerpts from
        pioneers, railroad schedules and advertisements, images of cowboys and
        pioneers, Chief Joseph's speech, land advertisements, and a westward
        movement map.

Phase 2 assessment. The assessment tasks are organized into two leveled Think-
Tac-Toe charts. To continue with the westward expansion theme, the Think-Tac-Toe
with the train image contains lower level tasks (see Figure 4.12), while the higher level
tasks are on the Think-Tac-Toe with the mountain image (see Figure 4.13). Teachers
should assign different charts based on students' readiness levels. Students should
pick an assessment task from two out of the three rows (maps, images and paintings,
and other primary sources).

***Phase 3: What does your group think about westward expansion? What evi-
dence leads you to this conclusion? (Choices of product based on learning styles).***
As a class, review the essential question for the unit: Was westward expansion good
for the United States?

Tasks. Students will do the following:

▪   Discuss the content you learned with everyone in your group; share ideas
    and facts using your westward expansion clue packet (see Figure 4.11). Once
    everyone in your group has the information from all sources in Phase 2, you
    may choose a partner for this part of the unit.
▪   Take a position on the essential question from your group's point of view. You
    may choose how you want to present your knowledge, but it must include
    evidence from sources to support your opinion. Refer to the preassessment
    for product choices. The product and partner choices must be approved by
    the teacher before you begin your work. Consult the DAP Tools or product
    rubrics as you create your project.

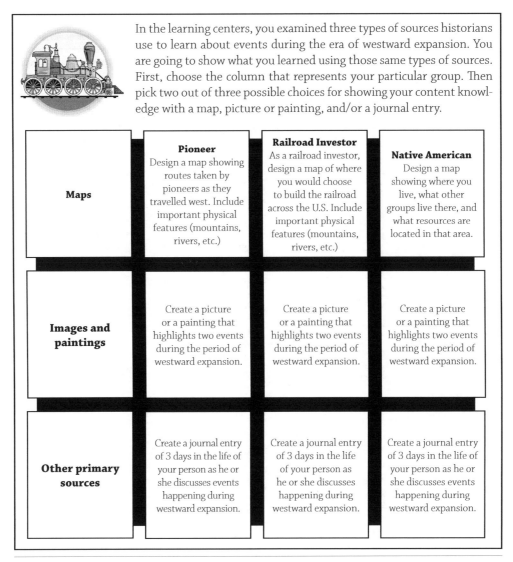

In the learning centers, you examined three types of sources historians use to learn about events during the era of westward expansion. You are going to show what you learned using those same types of sources. First, choose the column that represents your particular group. Then pick two out of three possible choices for showing your content knowledge with a map, picture or painting, and/or a journal entry.

	Pioneer	Railroad Investor	Native American
Maps	Design a map showing routes taken by pioneers as they travelled west. Include important physical features (mountains, rivers, etc.)	As a railroad investor, design a map of where you would choose to build the railroad across the U.S. Include important physical features (mountains, rivers, etc.)	Design a map showing where you live, what other groups live there, and what resources are located in that area.
Images and paintings	Create a picture or a painting that highlights two events during the period of westward expansion.	Create a picture or a painting that highlights two events during the period of westward expansion.	Create a picture or a painting that highlights two events during the period of westward expansion.
Other primary sources	Create a journal entry of 3 days in the life of your person as he or she discusses events happening during westward expansion.	Create a journal entry of 3 days in the life of your person as he or she discusses events happening during westward expansion.	Create a journal entry of 3 days in the life of your person as he or she discusses events happening during westward expansion.

Figure 4.12. Westward expansion Think-Tac-Toe, challenging.

When final products are complete, students can display all of the work for a museum walk around the room. This would be a great time to invite younger students to visit the fifth-grade classroom. Figures 4.14 and 4.15 are examples of student work from the westward expansion unit from Laureen Laumeyer's fifth-grade classroom at Meadow View Elementary in Radcliff, KY. As an individual assessment, students could complete a writing prompt where they answer the essential question with evidence from all of the phases of the lesson.

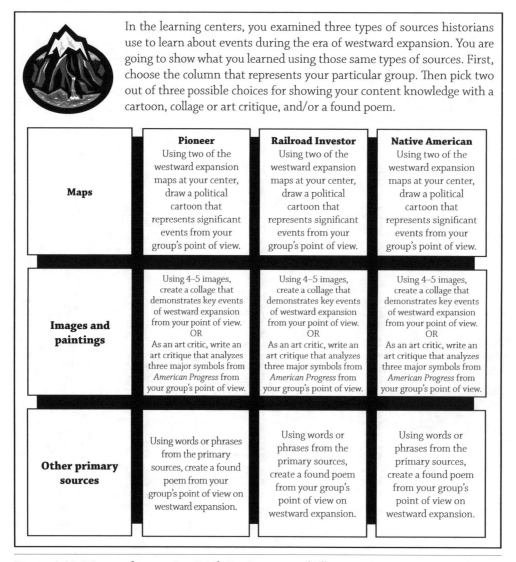

In the learning centers, you examined three types of sources historians use to learn about events during the era of westward expansion. You are going to show what you learned using those same types of sources. First, choose the column that represents your particular group. Then pick two out of three possible choices for showing your content knowledge with a cartoon, collage or art critique, and/or a found poem.

	Pioneer	**Railroad Investor**	**Native American**
Maps	Using two of the westward expansion maps at your center, draw a political cartoon that represents significant events from your group's point of view.	Using two of the westward expansion maps at your center, draw a political cartoon that represents significant events from your group's point of view.	Using two of the westward expansion maps at your center, draw a political cartoon that represents significant events from your group's point of view.
Images and paintings	Using 4–5 images, create a collage that demonstrates key events of westward expansion from your point of view. OR As an art critic, write an art critique that analyzes three major symbols from *American Progress* from your group's point of view.	Using 4–5 images, create a collage that demonstrates key events of westward expansion from your point of view. OR As an art critic, write an art critique that analyzes three major symbols from *American Progress* from your group's point of view.	Using 4–5 images, create a collage that demonstrates key events of westward expansion from your point of view. OR As an art critic, write an art critique that analyzes three major symbols from *American Progress* from your group's point of view.
Other primary sources	Using words or phrases from the primary sources, create a found poem from your group's point of view on westward expansion.	Using words or phrases from the primary sources, create a found poem from your group's point of view on westward expansion.	Using words or phrases from the primary sources, create a found poem from your group's point of view on westward expansion.

Figure 4.13. Westward expansion Think-Tac-Toe, more challenging.

CONCLUSION

By creating a classroom climate where differentiation is the norm and learning experiences are intentionally planned to meet students' needs, an energetic, diverse group of elementary or middle-school students can and will learn social studies! From heroes and wars, to ancient civilizations and the wild west, a differentiated social studies classroom can look like what Shoob and Stout (2008) described in *Teaching Social Studies Today*:

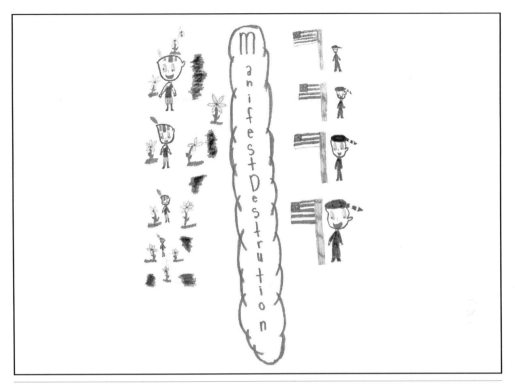

Figure 4.14. Political cartoon: "Manifest Destruction."

Figure 4.15. Political cartoon: "This Month . . . Many Months Later."

Observing an effective social studies classroom over a period of time would show different things going on every day: a variety of strategies appropriate to the learning, tasks/activities, and objectives. There would be an atmosphere that is engaging, challenging, stimulating, interactive, and thought provoking; lively and alive with student-centered learning, somewhat like a science laboratory. Members of the classroom would be respectful of others' points of view and appreciative of the benefits of diversity. The instruction would be relevant with purposeful learning that focuses on essential questions and understandings that link to other disciplines and the world beyond the classroom walls. A wide variety of resources, technology, visuals, and so on would be available as a means to tap into the varied learning styles of the students. The physical setup would be fluid and flexible and allow for meeting diverse learning needs and styles. Students would be engaged in reading, writing, observing, discussing, presenting, and researching. Collaboration among students would be the norm . . . Most of all, it would be fun! (pp. 14–15)

REFERENCES

Anderson, L. W., & Krathwohl, D. R. (Eds.). (2001). *A taxonomy for learning, teaching, and assessing: A revision of Bloom's taxonomy of educational objectives* (Abridged ed.). New York, NY: Longman.

Baicker, K. (2002). *The westward movement.* New York, NY: Scholastic.

Center for Civic Education. (2007). *National standards for civics and government.* Retrieved from http://www.civiced.org/index.php?page=stds

Coan, S. (Ed.). (2007). *Leveled texts for social studies: Expanding and preserving the Union.* Huntington Beach, CA: Shell Education.

Coil, C. (2004). *Standards-based activities and assessments for the differentiated classroom.* Marion, IL: Pieces of Learning.

Common Core State Standards Initiative. (2010). *Common core state standards for English language arts & literacy in history/social studies, science, and technical subjects.* Retrieved from http://www.corestandards.org/assets/CCSSI_ELA%20 Standards.pdf

Conklin, W. (2004). *Differentiation strategies for social studies.* Huntington Beach, CA: Shell Education.

Council for Economic Education. (2010). *Voluntary national content standards in economics.* Retrieved from http://www.councilforeconed.org/ea/program. php?pid=19

Denenberg, D., & Roscoe, L. (2006). *50 American heroes every kid should meet.* Minneapolis, MN: Millbrook Press.

Gardner, H. (1983). *Frames of mind: The theory of multiple intelligences.* New York, NY: Basic Books.

Karnes, F. A., & Stephens, K. (2009). *The ultimate guide for student product development and evaluation* (2nd ed.). Waco, TX: Prufrock Press.

Kirchner, J., Helm, A., Pierce, K., & Galloway, M. (2011, January/February). History + mystery = inquiring young historians: Experiences from a teaching American history grant. *Social Studies and the Young Learner,* 14–16.

National Center for History in the Schools. (1996). *United States history content standards for grades 5–12.* Retrieved from http://www.nchs.ucla.edu/Standards/us-history-content-standards

National Center for History in the Schools. (n.d.) *Basic principles—guiding the development of standards K–4.* Retrieved from http://www.nchs.ucla.edu/Standards/standards-for-grades-k-4/developing-standards-in-grades-k-4

National Council for the Social Studies. (2010). *National curriculum standards for social studies.* Retrieved from http://www.socialstudies.org/standards/strands

Parker, C. (2004). *Applying differentiation strategies.* Huntington Beach, CA: Shell Education.

Roberts, J. L., & Inman, T. F. (2009a). *Assessing differentiated student products: A protocol for development and evaluation.* Waco, TX: Prufrock Press.

Roberts, J. L., & Inman, T. F. (2009b). *Strategies for differentiating instruction: Best practices for the classroom* (2nd ed.). Waco, TX: Prufrock Press.

Shoob, S., & Stout, C. (2008). *Teaching social studies today.* Huntington Beach, CA: Shell Education.

Chapter 5

Science: Differentiation Through Agendas and Centers

Martha M. Day

*Equipped with his five senses, man explores the universe
around him and calls the adventure Science.*

—Edwin Powell Hubble

The use of centers and agendas in the science classroom allows the teacher to capitalize on students' innate curiosity about the natural world. Allowing students to interact with science content and processes through learning centers or agendas in ways that target their readiness levels, interests, and learning styles is truly representative of the nature of science. Scientists investigate problems that interest them and develop libraries of knowledge that are deeply connected to their fields of expertise. Why then shouldn't young scientists develop their research skills in the same manner? Developing a culture of inquiry in a science classroom allows students to make meaning from their experiences, resulting in ongoing changes in their mental frameworks (Osborne & Freyburg, 1985). Classrooms that show evidence of students engaged in science inquiry exhibit the following characteristics ("Inquiry-Based Science: What Does it Look Like?," 1995):

- Children view themselves as scientists in the process of learning.
    - They look forward to doing science.
    - They demonstrate a desire to learn more.
    - They seek to collaborate and work cooperatively with their peers.
    - They are confident in doing science; they demonstrate a willingness to modify ideas, take risks, and display healthy skepticism.

- Children accept an "invitation to learn" and readily engage in the exploration process.
    - Children exhibit curiosity and ponder observations.

- o They move around selecting and using the materials they need.
- o They take the opportunity and the time to "try out" their own ideas.

- Children plan and carry out investigations.
  - o Children design a way to try out their ideas, not expecting to be told what to do.
  - o They plan ways to verify, extend, or discard ideas.
  - o They carry out investigations by handling materials, observing, measuring, and recording data.

- Children communicate using a variety of methods.
  - o Children express ideas in a variety of ways: journals, reporting out, drawing, graphing, and charting.
  - o They listen, speak, and write about science with parents, teachers, and peers.
  - o They use the language of the processes of science.
  - o They communicate their level of understanding of concepts that they have developed to date.

- Children propose explanations and solutions and build a store of concepts.
  - o Children offer explanations from a "store" of previous knowledge.
  - o They use investigations to satisfy their own questions.
  - o They sort out information and decide what is important.
  - o They are willing to revise explanations as they gain new knowledge.

- Children raise questions.
  - o Children ask questions (verbally or through actions).
  - o They use questions to lead them to investigations that generate further questions or ideas.
  - o Children value and enjoy asking questions as an important part of science.

- Children use observation.
  - o Children observe, as opposed to just looking.
  - o They see details, they detect sequences and events, and they notice change, similarities, and differences.
  - o They make connections to previously held ideas.

- Children critique their science practices.
  - o They use indicators to assess their own work.
  - o They report their strengths and weaknesses.

○ They reflect with their peers. (p. 35)

Because students enter the science classroom with a broad range of academic needs, teachers are charged with the task of finding ways to structure lessons to accommodate academically diverse populations. Elementary and middle grade science teachers can create equitable learning experiences for students from different socioeconomic, cultural, linguistic, and physiological backgrounds through the use of differentiated instruction.

Centers and agendas are only useful in differentiating instruction if state and national science standards are addressed within the content presented. Most states currently align their science content standards with the National Science Education Standards (NSES; National Research Council, 1996). In the next year, the majority of states will adopt the Common Core Standards for science curricula. At the time of this writing, only a preliminary draft of the Common Core Standards for science was available. All of the centers and agendas in this chapter directly address one of the life science, Earth/space science, physical science, or engineering and technology standards. Further, each of the lessons presented include cross-cutting elements of major ideas that have application across all domains of science. Teachers can differentiate content, process, and/or product for students in the science classroom (Tomlinson, 1999). Differentiation of content by student interest entails a change in the material being learned by the student. If the teacher's learning goal is for all students to demonstrate a working knowledge of the scientific method, some of the students may design an experiment, explicitly outlining the steps in the scientific method, while others may review an experiment that has already been completed and look for specific pieces of evidence that demonstrate the steps of the scientific method. Differentiation of process via ability and readiness involves providing student choice with various avenues in which the learning is accessed. For example, some students may be asked to explore centers designed to facilitate student learning on force and motion, with each center focusing on a different level of Bloom's taxonomy. Differentiation of product relates to the manner in which students demonstrate what they have learned. For example, the teacher could allow students to choose from a menu of activities that enable students to demonstrate understanding of plant and animal cells. Some students may choose to create analogies of cellular organelles to parts of a city, others may choose to build models of the cell, and still others may choose to develop a social media site for the cell.

The science lessons contained in this chapter are organized by differentiation of content, process, and product, and each section contains three examples: one for grades K–2, one for grades 3–5, and one for grades 6–8. Because the very nature of science instruction entails building on existing knowledge, each lesson could be easily modified for another grade level. All differentiated instruction should begin with a preassessment activity to assist both the learner and teacher in determining the learner's instructional learning style, interest, and readiness level.

CONTENT DIFFERENTIATION BASED ON STUDENT INTEREST

Differentiation of science content based on student interest involves identifying topics that the student may want to explore or activities that will motivate the student to engage in the lesson. Although each student is still responsible for learning key facets of the content, targeting student interest can create an environment where students are willing to take charge of their own learning. The following examples illustrate ways to differentiate content based on the interests of students.

Digging Up Details on Worms (Grade 2)

Standard Addressed: NSES K–4 Life Science Content Standard C: The characteristics of organisms.

Lesson Hook: Ask students to share information that they know about worms. Encourage students to discuss their experiences, observations, and feelings about worms. Have students share any questions they have about worms. Record the students' responses on chart paper.

Assignment: The purpose of this task is for students to investigate the characteristics of worms and the habitats they live in. Students visit centers that contain books about worms appropriate to students' reading levels. Once students have chosen a nonfiction book, they should select options from the menu (see Figure 5.1) to complete. The centers should also include enrichment such as pictures of worms and worm habitats from magazines, access to computers for students to complete research on worms, and art supplies.

Exploring the Cell (Grade 5)

Standard Addressed: NSES 5–8 Life Science Content Standard C: Structure and function in living systems.

Lesson Hook: What are things that every city needs in order to operate? Ask students to write their answers to this question and to share their answers with the class. How do the things that a city needs to operate compare with what a plant or an animal cell

Appetizer: Pick One

_____ 1. Make four trading cards with worm characteristics.

_____ 2. Write and sing a song with four facts about worms.

Main Dish: Pick One
What are the most important things that a worm needs in its environment to live? Answer in one of these products. You must include evidence!

_____ 1. Travel brochure

_____ 2. Photo story

_____ 3. Diorama

Side Dish: Pick Two

_____ 1. Write a journal entry from a worm's perspective.

_____ 2. Create a collage of 3 characteristics of worms.

_____ 3. Write a script of a conversation between two worms looking for food.

_____ 4. Design a comic strip showing the activities of a worm family.

Dessert: (Optional)

_____ 1. Create a bumper sticker that shows a detail about a worm.

_____ 2. Design a T-shirt that illustrates a characteristic of a worm.

Figure 5.1. Menu: Characteristics of worms. Adapted from "History + Mystery = Inquiring Young Historians: Experiences From a Teaching American History Grant" by J. Kirchner, A. Helm, K. Pierce, & M. Galloway, 2011, January/February, _Social Studies and the Young Learner_, pp. P3–P4. Copyright 2011 by National Council for the Social Studies. Adapted with permission.

needs to operate? Ask students to write their answers to this question and to share their answers with the class.

Assignment: Students will choose to investigate either the parts of an animal cell or those of a plant cell. Students will then work in centers, individually or in groups, to address the agenda tasks (see Figure 5.2) to create a travel brochure that describes a plant or an animal cell as if the cell were a city or other attraction such as a zoo, farm, shopping mall, or ball park. Centers need to have books and computers available for research. Teachers may elect to use a DAP Tool to assess the final student product.

My Favorite Scientist (Grade 7)

Standard Addressed: NSES 5–8 History and Nature of Science Content Standard G: Science as a human endeavor and history of science; Science in Personal and Social Perspectives Content Standard F: Science and technology in society.

Lesson Hook: What type of person do you imagine when you hear the word "scientist"? Visualize a scientist in your mind and then draw that person on paper. Then, in 50 words, describe what it means to be a scientist. Teachers should lead a discussion based on the students' responses. Then, the entire class should brainstorm important inventions, scientific discoveries, and famous scientists.

Assignment: Students will choose a scientist to research. After the students choose their scientist, they will work in centers to research that person and his or her contributions to advancing the body of scientific knowledge in society (see Figure 5.3). The teacher should provide trade books, computers with Internet access, and art supplies so that students can create products to demonstrate their knowledge.

DIFFERENTIATION OF PROCESS VIA ABILITY AND READINESS (BLOOM AND PREASSESSMENTS)

An effective method to foster and encourage the growth of all students in a classroom is to differentiate activities through tiered assignments based on individual students' levels of readiness and ability. Tiering can be based on the challenge level, complexity, resources used, outcome, process, or product (Heacox, 2002). Tiered assignments involve students completing different types of work to reflect mastery of content objectives. Although tiered assignments vary, the assignments should be similar in their engagement and activity levels as well as equitable in terms of work expectations and time needed to complete the activities. The following examples use Think-Tac-Toes, Bloom charts, and centers based on the revised Bloom's taxonomy

Your Task: You will produce a travel brochure that describes a plant or animal cell as if it were some type of travel attraction such as a shopping mall, ballpark, amusement park, city, farm, hotel, ski resort, museum, art gallery, and so forth. Once you have chosen a type of cell and type of attraction, you are to collect background information about the cell. You may use books or online resources to research facts about your plant or animal cell and type of attraction. Include the following information:

- The front cover of the brochure should include the name of your attraction and a graphic of your choice. Remember, you are trying to attract people to visit your cell so be sure that your cover is eye-catching and creative.
- The back cover of the brochure should contain a labeled diagram of your entire cell with fictional directions to the cell.
- The interior panels of your brochure should include descriptions of the structure and function of at least eight cell organelles using creative comparisons to show what part would be at your attraction. Example: *While visiting our hotel, please remember to turn our mitochondria off to conserve energy when it is not needed.*
- Include a real graphic of every part of the attraction you use as well as a graphic of what it is at your cell. Example: *A graphic of a light switch plate at the hotel and a graphic of the mitochondria*
- Please use appropriate grammar and spelling in your brochure.

Your Product: Create a trifold, six-panel paper or digital travel brochure that will persuade visitors to travel to your special attraction to investigate the wonders of cells.

Figure 5.2. Agenda for Exploring the Cell center.

(Anderson & Krathwohl, 2001). A key factor in using these tools effectively is for teachers to preassess students' ability and readiness levels prior to making assignments.

States of Matter (Grade K)

Standards Addressed: NSES K–4 Physical Science Content Standard B: Properties of Objects and Materials; Science as Inquiry Content Standard A: Abilities necessary to do scientific inquiry and understandings about scientific inquiry.

Lesson Hook: Read and discuss *Solids, Liquids, and Gases* by Ginger Garrett (2005) with basic level learners to investigate properties of matter. Read and discuss *What Is the World Made of? All About Solids, Liquids and Gases* by Kathleen Weidner Zoehfeld and Paul Meisel (1998) with students who need a higher level of complexity with the investigation of properties of matter.

Assignment: Students should work at tiered centers to investigate the properties of matter. Prior to giving the Bloom tasks in Figure 5.4 to the students, the teacher should separate the Bloom chart into handout strips and position the tasks at vari-

Your Task: Choose a scientist to investigate as your favorite scientist. Once you choose your favorite scientist, use books, library resources, and the Internet to research information about that person. Uncover the following information:

- A picture of your favorite scientist and a picture or illustration of the scientist's major discoveries or inventions
- The scientist's date of birth and a description of where the scientist grew up and went to school
- Reasons why the scientist chose to study in his or her particular field of study
- The scientist's major discoveries or inventions and how the discoveries impacted society
- Two interesting facts about the scientist
- Things that the scientist or inventor likes to do in his or her spare time
- Two reasons for choosing this scientist as your favorite scientist

Your Product: Choose one of these products to create and share your information with the class:

- Write a persuasive, business-style letter to the Nobel Prize selection committee, explaining why your favorite scientist should receive a Nobel Prize for his or her discovery or invention. Include a picture of your favorite scientist and illustrations of the scientist's discoveries and/or inventions as addendums to your letter.
- Design a prezi, PowerPoint presentation, or trifold display poster of your favorite scientist that includes the information listed above.
- Create a dodecahedron manipulative of your favorite scientist that includes the information listed above.
- Write a five-stanza song, create a mask in the likeness of the scientist, and make props that represent the scientist's discovery or invention. Perform your song wearing the mask and using the props you created.

Figure 5.3. Agenda for My Favorite Scientist center.

ous learning centers to level the learning tasks. The teacher may choose to divide the chart into three sections, remember/understand, apply/analyze, and evaluate/create. This strategy would provide opportunities for two choices of tasks at three different levels of cognitive complexity.

A Matter of Heart (Grade 3)

Standards Addressed: NSES K–4 Science in Personal and Social Perspectives Content Standard F: Personal health; History and the Nature of Science Content Standard G: Science as a human endeavor.

Lesson Hook: The teacher should show students a stethoscope and ask, "How does a stethoscope make sounds louder?" Next, the teacher should record student responses on chart paper. Read the article "A Doctor's Quest" by Gloria Wagner (2002) to stu-

	PROCESS	CONTENT	PRODUCT
CREATE	Create	Properties of Matter	Drawing
	Create a toy that uses at least two states of matter.		
EVALUATE	Justify	Properties of Matter	Oral Presentation
	Decide which state of matter would be best for filling a balloon or washing your dog. Tell why.		
ANALYZE	Organize	Properties of Matter	Chart
	Classify objects in the classroom into gas, liquid, or solid groups.		
APPLY	Show	Properties of Matter	Collage
	Show examples of each state of matter using magazine pictures.		
UNDERSTAND	Define	Properties of Matter	Flash Cards
	Explain each of the three states of matter and illustrate each.		
REMEMBER	List	Properties of Matter	Poster
	List the three states of matter and give an example of each.		

Figure 5.4. Grade 4: Bloom chart—Properties of Matter. Used with permission by Julia L. Roberts and Tracy Ford Inman, Western Kentucky University.

dents. Ask students to try making a stethoscope of their own using a cardboard tube from a paper towel roll. Have students pair up and listen for their partner's heartbeat by placing the tube over their partner's heart and counting the number of beats heard over a 30-second period. Students should add this number together twice to get the number of heartbeats per minute. The partner should then run in place for one minute and the process of counting heart beats should be repeated to see if the number changes after exercise. The partners should switch roles and repeat the experiment.

Assignment: Students should work at tiered centers using a Bloom chart (see Figure 5.5) to investigate the characteristics of the human heart. The teacher should separate the Bloom chart into handout strips and position the tasks at various learning centers to level the learning tasks.

Elements, Compounds, and Mixtures (Grade 6)

Standard Addressed: NSES 5–8 Physical Science Content Standard B: Properties and changes of properties of matter.

Lesson Hook: Ask students to do a prewriting assignment explaining the differences among elements, compounds, and mixtures. The prewriting assignment will also serve as a preassessment to assist the teacher in grouping students during the task.

Assignment: Students should complete the Think-Tac-Toe agenda (see Figures 5.6 and 5.7) as their final assessment to demonstrate their understanding of elements, compounds, and mixtures. The teacher may decide whether to have the students complete all of the activities or to select a specified number of activities to complete from the agenda. Although there are two levels of the task, the content covered is similar. The activities differ only in the level of process skill required to complete the task.

DIFFERENTIATION OF PRODUCT VIA LEARNING STYLE/MULTIPLE INTELLIGENCES (THINK-TAC-TOE)

Differentiating instruction to appeal to various learning styles and multiple intelligences can serve as powerful motivators in a classroom. Differentiating based on product development requires the application of a wide variety of assessment strategies and offers students a choice of projects that reflect a wide variety of learning styles and interests. Product differentiation affords students many different methods to demonstrate what has been learned.

The following three examples are based on two different approaches: learning styles based on Roberts and Inman (2009b) and multiple intelligences as explored in

	PROCESS	CONTENT	PRODUCT
CREATE	Create	The Human Heart	Invention
	Create a simple apparatus that allows you to detect a human heartbeat.		
EVALUATE	Experiment	The Human Heart	Laboratory Report
	Hypothesize on which activity makes your heart beat faster: 30 seconds of running, 30 seconds of hopping, or 30 seconds of jumping jacks. Experiment to support your hypothesis, record your data, and write the results in a laboratory report.		
ANALYZE	Research	The Human Heart	Newspaper Article
	Research two diseases that affect the human heart. Write a newspaper article that compares the two diseases.		
APPLY	Determine	The Human Heart	Diagram
	Make a labeled diagram of the human heart to trace the flow of blood through the heart and lungs.		
UNDERSTAND	Illustrate	The Human Heart	Drawing
	In your own words, describe the function of the four chambers of the heart.		
REMEMBER	List	The Human Heart	Poster
	Color and label the parts of a diagram of the heart.		

Figure 5.5. Grade 3: Bloom chart—A Matter of Heart. Used with permission by Julia L. Roberts and Tracy Ford Inman, Western Kentucky University.

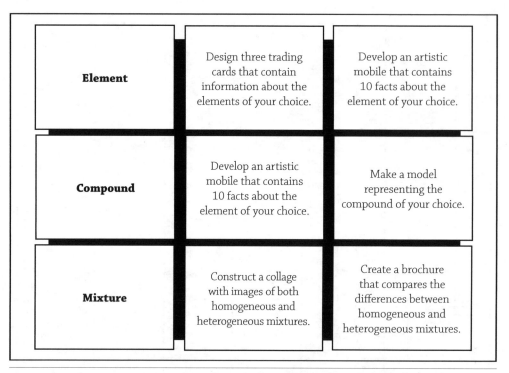

Figure 5.6. Elements, Compounds, and Mixtures challenging Think-Tac-Toe.

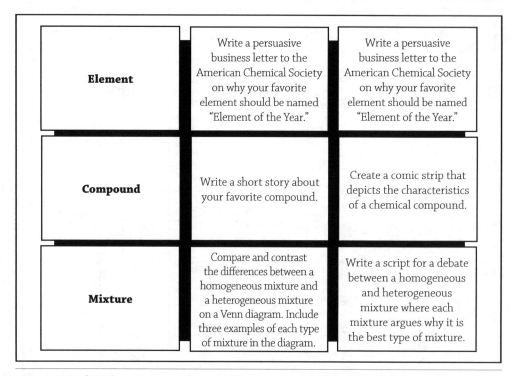

Figure 5.7. Elements, Compounds, and Mixtures more challenging Think-Tac-Toe.

Gardner's (1983) *Frames of Mind: The Theory of Multiple Intelligences*. When creating these types of assignments, it is important to include at least one option for each type of intelligence and learning style.

Technology All Around (Grade 1)

Standard Addressed: NSES K–4 Science and Technology Content Standard E: Understanding of science and technology.

Lesson Hook: Ask students to provide examples of how we use technology. Humans have always had problems and have invented tools and techniques to solve problems. Explain that technology is the application of any tool or knowledge that improves our quality of life. Record the students' answers on chart paper.

Assignment: Allow students to choose a learning center from those listed below to investigate a form of technology. At the conclusion of the investigation, use the Technology All Around Think-Tac-Toe (see Figure 5.8) to allow students to demonstrate what was learned during their investigation.

- *Center 1: All in the Balance:* Read the book *Mirette on a High Wire* by Emily McCully (1992). Discuss the many ways that Mirette was able to balance. Provide students with a paper clip and a small Styrofoam cube. Ask students to design and construct an object that will balance on their finger. The paper clip should be pushed into the cube and should be the only item that comes into contact with the student's finger. Students should use trial and error to make discoveries about balance and center of gravity. Ask students to brainstorm about machines that require balance in order to operate.
- *Center 2: Muddy Waters:* Read the book *Dirt Boy* by Erik Slangerup (2000). Ask the students to guess what materials might be left in the bathwater after someone takes a bath. Show students a jar of muddy water and ask the students to predict ways to clean the water. Provide students with a cup of muddy water, an empty cup, cotton balls, and two additional cups with holes poked in the sides. Ask the students to try to build a device to clean the water and have them discuss their results.
- *Center 3: The Butter Battle:* Begin by reading *The Butter Battle Book* by Dr. Seuss (1984). Discuss the book and ways to reunite the Zooks and Yooks described in the book. Ask students to divide into two small groups to each invent a new way to eat butter. Each group (Zooks and Yooks) will need a large glass jar with a lid (spaghetti jars work well), one 250 mL carton of heavy cream, pieces of bread, paper plates, plastic knives, and napkins. Provide students with a set of instructions on how to make butter: (1) Pour the cream into the jar and screw the lid on tightly. (2) Sit down and take turns shaking the

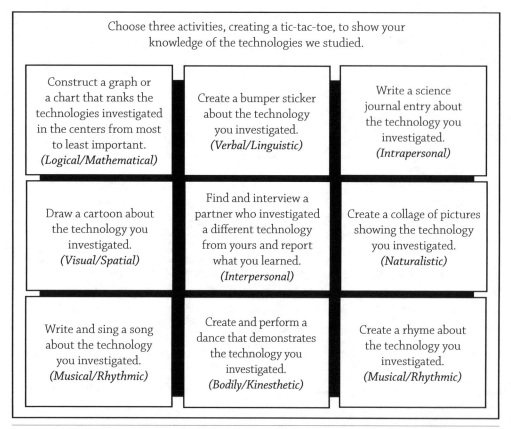

Figure 5.8. Technology All Around Think-Tac-Toe.

jar. (3) Shake until butter forms, about 15 minutes. (4) Carefully pour off and discard the white liquid (buttermilk) and put the butter on a plate. (5) Distribute the bread, butter, plates, and knives and invent your new way to eat butter.

- *Center 4: The Marshmallow Machine*: Begin by telling the group that they are going to become a marshmallow-smashing machine. Each person in the group will be a "cog" in the machine to smash the marshmallows by creating a movement or a sound in the marshmallow smashing process. Provide the group with three or four marshmallows so that they can demonstrate their machine. After the students demonstrate their machine, read the story *Mike Mulligan and His Steam Shovel* by Virginia Burton (1967). Ask the students to point out the parts that make up the steam shovel and to think of other machines that have many parts.

Solar System

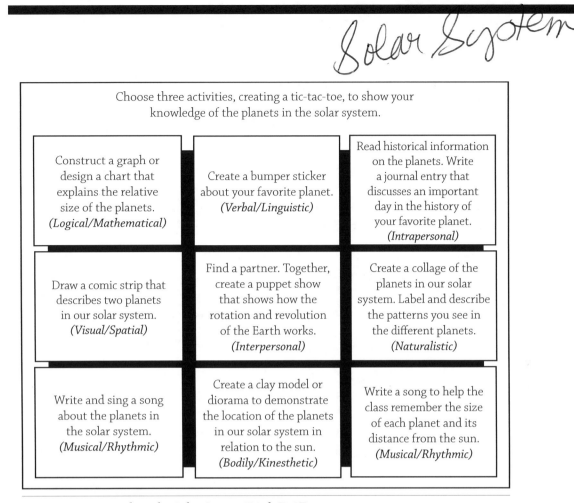

Choose three activities, creating a tic-tac-toe, to show your knowledge of the planets in the solar system.

Construct a graph or design a chart that explains the relative size of the planets. *(Logical/Mathematical)*	Create a bumper sticker about your favorite planet. *(Verbal/Linguistic)*	Read historical information on the planets. Write a journal entry that discusses an important day in the history of your favorite planet. *(Intrapersonal)*
Draw a comic strip that describes two planets in our solar system. *(Visual/Spatial)*	Find a partner. Together, create a puppet show that shows how the rotation and revolution of the Earth works. *(Interpersonal)*	Create a collage of the planets in our solar system. Label and describe the patterns you see in the different planets. *(Naturalistic)*
Write and sing a song about the planets in the solar system. *(Musical/Rhythmic)*	Create a clay model or diorama to demonstrate the location of the planets in our solar system in relation to the sun. *(Bodily/Kinesthetic)*	Write a song to help the class remember the size of each planet and its distance from the sun. *(Musical/Rhythmic)*

Figure 5.9. The Earth in the Solar System Think-Tac-Toe.

The Earth in the Solar System (Grade 4)

Standard Addressed: NSES K–4 Earth Science Content Standard D: Objects in the sky; changes in the Earth and sky.

Lesson Hook: Ask students the following questions: Do you know how many planets there are in our solar system? Can you tell me some of the colors of the planets? Is Earth (our planet) any different from others? Record the class' responses on chart paper and discuss the responses. Use the discussion as a springboard to introduce the planets in our solar system.

Assignment: Students will explore the planets in our solar system by conducting research either independently or in groups. Each student or group is responsible for choosing one activity from each of the three horizontal rows of the Think-Tac-Toe chart in Figure 5.9 to demonstrate their knowledge of the planets in our solar system.

The Periodic Table (Grade 8)

Standard Addressed: NSES 5–8 Physical Science Content Standard B: Properties and changes of properties of matter.

Lesson Hook: Ask students to brainstorm all of the things they can think of that must be organized in order to function effectively and to be useful to society. Record the class' responses on chart paper and discuss the responses. Use the discussion as a springboard to introduce the periodic table.

Assignment: Students will explore the periodic table by conducting research either independently or in groups. Each student or group is responsible for choosing one activity from each of the three horizontal rows of the Think-Tac-Toe chart in Figure 5.10 to demonstrate their knowledge of the periodic table.

PUTTING IT ALL TOGETHER: CONTENT, PROCESS, AND DIFFERENTIATION (WITH PREASSESSMENT)

We have explored differentiation in science through content, process, and product in individual components. Now it is time to combine all three differentiation strategies into one lesson. It is not necessary to combine the three strategies within the context of every lesson you teach but some science concepts are well suited to this format. Combining the three differentiation strategies can also serve to create a diverse learning community within your classroom.

Biomes (Grade 5)

Standards Addressed: NSES 5–8 Science as Inquiry Content Standard A: Abilities necessary to do scientific inquiry, understandings about scientific inquiry; Physical Science Content Standard C: Populations and ecosystems; diversity and adaptations of organisms.

Lesson Overview: This lesson is part of a unit on ecosystems and animal environments. Students will have completed a unit on the basic needs of living things and should be familiar with vocabulary terms such as ecosystem, ocean, desert, tundra, animal, habitat, survival, consumer, producer, decomposer, and adaptation.

Preassessment: A preassessment (see Figure 5.11) allows the teacher to effectively assign students to the most appropriate content level, process option, and product.

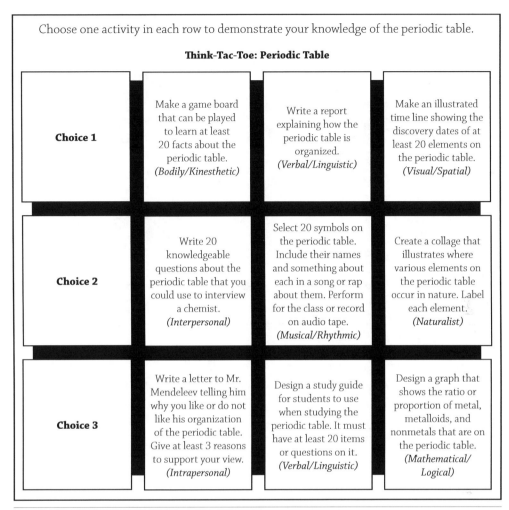

Choose one activity in each row to demonstrate your knowledge of the periodic table.

Think-Tac-Toe: Periodic Table

Choice 1	Make a game board that can be played to learn at least 20 facts about the periodic table. *(Bodily/Kinesthetic)*	Write a report explaining how the periodic table is organized. *(Verbal/Linguistic)*	Make an illustrated time line showing the discovery dates of at least 20 elements on the periodic table. *(Visual/Spatial)*
Choice 2	Write 20 knowledgeable questions about the periodic table that you could use to interview a chemist. *(Interpersonal)*	Select 20 symbols on the periodic table. Include their names and something about each in a song or rap about them. Perform for the class or record on audio tape. *(Musical/Rhythmic)*	Create a collage that illustrates where various elements on the periodic table occur in nature. Label each element. *(Naturalist)*
Choice 3	Write a letter to Mr. Mendeleev telling him why you like or do not like his organization of the periodic table. Give at least 3 reasons to support your view. *(Intrapersonal)*	Design a study guide for students to use when studying the periodic table. It must have at least 20 items or questions on it. *(Verbal/Linguistic)*	Design a graph that shows the ratio or proportion of metal, metalloids, and nonmetals that are on the periodic table. *(Mathematical/ Logical)*

Figure 5.10. The Periodic Table Think-Tac-Toe. From *Strategies for Differentiating Instruction: Best Practices for the Classroom* (2nd ed., p. 236), by J. L. Roberts and T. F. Inman, 2009, Waco, TX: Prufrock Press. Copyright 2009 Prufrock Press. Reprinted with permission.

Differentiation of Content: This lesson on ecosystems and animal habitats is categorized according to student interest. The teacher may allow students to have free choice as to which category is studied or the teacher may assign students to categories based on the information gathered from the preassessment activity. This lesson allows students to expand the basic information learned about ecosystems and animal environments by broadening their depth of knowledge on specific animal environments and ecosystems. The categories are as follows: Category I: Desert, Category II: Ocean, and Category III: Tundra.

Content:

1. Where would you most like to go on a vacation? (Circle one)

   Snowy landscape   Desert landscape   Ocean landscape

2. Which type of animal interests you the most? (Circle one)

   Shark   Polar bear   Lizard

Process: You may use the back of this page for Questions 3 and 4, if necessary.

3. Explain what an animal needs to survive in its environment.
4. Summarize what is meant by "survival of the fittest."

Product:

5. Circle those products that you have created before.
6. Put a star beside those products that interest you that you have not created before.

Diorama	Mask	Model	Sculpture
Debate	Interview	Monologue	Oral Presentation
Computer Graphic	Movie	Podcast	PowerPoint
Cartoon	Collage	Pamphlet	Poster
Diary	Essay	Letter	Written Interview

Figure 5.11. Ecosystems and animal environments preassessment.

Differentiation of Process: Based on the results from the preassessment, students will receive one of two assignment sheets (see Figures 5.12 and 5.13). Each assignment sheet contains two options for students, but one assignment sheet focuses on Bloom's lower cognitive levels while the other assignment sheet focuses on Bloom's higher cognitive levels. Each assignment contains a grand challenge on ecosystems and animal habitats. Students are offered three options to "go public" with their newfound knowledge of ecosystems and animal habitats.

Differentiation of Product: Students may choose any product from the product list to demonstrate their knowledge of ecosystems and animal environments. Teachers must provide adequate instruction to ensure that students know how to create the product that they choose and teachers must find a time-efficient and appropriate method to assess the wide variety of product choices. DAP Tools are extremely

---

Ecosystems and Animal Environments

Each of you has selected an ecosystem and animal environment to study based on your interests. There are three parts to this assignment: (1) your initial ideas about the grand challenge, (2) a project selected from the two options below, and (3) a go public product selected from the product list to showcase your work. *Please remember to ask the teacher for a rubric after you make your project and product selections.

The Grand Challenge

You have just watched a very disturbing news report. Your favorite ecosystem has just been polluted because of a terrible oil spill. Rescue teams are going to the spill site to try to help the animals whose habitats are threatened because of the oil spill. You want to help by presenting as much information as possible about the unique needs of the animals in the ecosystem to the rescue teams before their departure.

What are your initial ideas on how to research this problem?

What background knowledge is needed?

Project Choices

Select a project from one of the two choices below.

- Describe at least five types of animals that live in your habitat and list the things that each of the animals eats. Create a summary of at least four facts about your chosen ecosystem that make it different from other ecosystems. (Bloom's levels Remember/Understand)
- Select at least five different types of animals that live in your chosen ecosystem. Classify these animals as herbivores, carnivores, or omnivores. Explain the unique characteristics of your chosen ecosystem. (Bloom's levels Apply/Understand)

Product Choices: Go Public With Your Newfound Knowledge!

See the product choices list. Be sure to get a rubric from the teacher once you have selected your product.

Figure 5.12. Agenda for Biomes center, challenging.

---

efficient for assessment for two reasons: (1) DAP Tools are predeveloped for a wide variety of product choices, and (2) DAP Tools are created at three different tier levels, thus allowing for differentiation in levels of challenge with the product created (Roberts & Inman, 2009b). Teachers may also choose to design their own rubrics to accompany the products. If this is the case, the teacher should distribute the rubrics to the students at the onset of the assignment. The sample product list in Figure 5.14 incorporates activities to accommodate the various learning preferences but limits student choices to those with DAP Tools (see Roberts & Inman, 2009a, for more on DAP Tools).

Ecosystems and Animal Environments

Each of you has selected an ecosystem and animal environment to study based on your interests. There are three parts to this assignment: (1) your initial ideas about the grand challenge, (2) a project selected from the two options below, and (3) a go public product selected from the product list to showcase your work. *Please remember to ask the teacher for a rubric after you make your project and product selections.

The Grand Challenge

You have just watched a very disturbing news report. Your favorite ecosystem has just been polluted because of a terrible oil spill. Rescue teams are going to the spill site to try to help the animals whose habitats are threatened because of the oil spill. You want to help by presenting as much information as possible about the unique needs of the animals in the ecosystem to the rescue teams before their departure.

What are your initial ideas on how to research this problem?

What background knowledge is needed?

Project Choices

Select a project from one of the two choices below.

- Organize at least five types of animals that live in your habitat into three categories (herbivore, omnivore, or carnivore) and provide two food requirements for each animal. Provide justification for the four most critical habitat requirements for the animals that live in this ecosystem. (Bloom's levels Analyze/Evaluate)
- Produce an alternative environment that five animals in your chosen ecosystem could adapt to if the rescuers had to move the animals to a zoo or sanctuary. Rank the three most important habitat requirements needed for each animal to survive. (Bloom's levels Evaluate/Create)

Product Choices: Go Public With Your Newfound Knowledge!

See the product choices list. Be sure to get a rubric from the teacher once you have selected your product.

Figure 5.13. Agenda for Biomes center, more challenging.

FINAL THOUGHTS

Differentiated instruction requires thoughtful lesson planning and acknowledgement that diverse student abilities and interests have a major impact on learning. In a differentiated classroom, variance occurs in the way in which students gain access to the content being taught (Hall, Strangman, & Meyer, 2003). The greatest benefit offered by differentiated instruction is that it enables the teacher to maximize the growth of each student by addressing their specific instructional needs. And what could be more important than each child, in every classroom, making appropriate and continuous progress in learning?

Product List			
Kinesthetic Products:			
Diorama	Mask	Model	Sculpture
Oral Products:			
Debate	Interview	Monologue	Oral Presentation
Technological Products:			
Computer Graphic	Movie	Podcast	PowerPoint
Visual Products:			
Cartoon	Collage	Pamphlet	Poster
Written Products:			
Diary	Essay	Letter	Written Interview

Figure 5.14. Product list for Biomes center.

CHAPTER 5 RESOURCES

The 8 Planets, Just for Kids—http://kids.nineplanets.org

All About Astronomy—http://www.enchantedlearning.com/subjects/astronomy

Animals and Pets—http://kids.nationalgeographic.com/kids/animals/creaturefeature

Cells Are the Starting Point—http://www.biology4kids.com/files/cell_main.html

Common Core State Standards Initiative—http://www.corestandards.org

Compounds and Mixtures—http://www.brainpop.com/science/matterandchemistry/compoundsandmixtures

Development of the Periodic Table—http://web.fccj.org/~ethall/period/period.htm

Dynamic Periodic Table—http://www.ptable.com

Elements, Compounds, & Mixtures— http://www.chem.purdue.edu/gchelp/atoms/elements.html

Eukaryotic Cell Interactive Animation—http://cellsalive.com/cells/cell_model.htm

Habitats: Simplified Explanations—http://wwf.panda.org/about_our_earth/ecoregions/about/habitat_types/habitats

How the Heart Works: Blood Flow Diagram—http://childrensheartinstitute.org/educate/heartwrk/bloodflw.htm

Hydrogen—http://www.rsc.org/chemsoc/visualelements/pages/hydrogen.html

Ice, Water & Steam—http://www.youtube.com/watch?v=QLXPfz8EkzM

Inventor of the Week Archive—http://web.mit.edu/invent/i-archive.html

Label Heart Interior Anatomy Diagram—http://www.enchantedlearning.com/subjects/anatomy/heart/labelinterior/label.shtml

Make a Dodecahedron—http://www.enchantedlearning.com/math/geometry/solids/Dodecahedrontemp.shtml

The Official Website of the Nobel Prize—http://nobelprize.org

Welcome to the Planets—http://pds.nasa.gov/planets/welcome.htm

REFERENCES

Anderson, L. W., & Krathwohl, D. R. (Eds.). (2001). *A taxonomy for learning, teaching, and assessing: A revision of Bloom's taxonomy of educational objectives* (Abridged ed.). New York, NY: Longman.

Burton, V. (1967). *Mike Mulligan and his steam shovel.* Orlando, FL: Sandpiper Houghton Mifflin.

Gardner, H. (1983). *Frames of mind: The theory of multiple intelligences.* New York, NY: Basic Books.

Garrett, G. (2005). *Solids, liquids and gases.* New York, NY: Children's Press.

Hall, T., Strangman, N., & Meyer, A. (2003). *Differentiated instruction and implications for UDL implementation.* Retrieved from http://www.k8accesscenter.org/training_resources/udl/diffinstruction.asp

Heacox, D. (2002). *Differentiating instruction in the regular classroom.* Minneapolis, MN: Free Sprit.

Inquiry based science: What does it look like? (1995, March–April). *Connect, 35.*

Kirchner, J., Helm, A., Pierce, K., & Galloway, M. (2011, January/February). History + mystery = inquiring young historians: Experiences from a teaching American history grant. *Social Studies and the Young Learner, 14–16.*

McCully, E. (1992). *Mirette on the high wire.* New York, NY: Scholastic.

National Research Council. (1996). *National science education standards.* Washington, DC: National Academy Press.

Osborne, M., & Freyberg, P. (1985). *Learning in science: Implications of children's knowledge.* Auckland, New Zealand: Heinemann.

Roberts, J. L., & Inman, T. F. (2009a). *Assessing differentiated student products: A protocol for development and evaluation.* Waco, TX: Prufrock Press.

Roberts, J. L., & Inman, T. F. (2009b). *Strategies for differentiating instruction: Best practices for the classroom* (2nd ed.). Waco, TX: Prufrock Press.

Seuss, D. (1984). *The butter battle book.* New York, NY: Random House.

Slangerup, E. (2000). *Dirt boy.* Park Ridge, IL: Albert Whitman and Company.

Tomlinson, C. A. (1999). *How to differentiate instruction in mixed-ability classrooms.* Alexandria, VA: ASCD.

Wagner, G. (2002). A doctor's quest. *Child Life, 81,* 20–21.

Zoehfeld, K. W., & Meisel, P. (1998). *What is the world made of? All about solids, liquids, and gases.* New York, NY: Collins.

Math Centers and Agendas

Janet Lynne Tassell

Pure mathematics is the world's best game. It is more absorbing than chess, more of a gamble than poker, and lasts longer than Monopoly. It's free. It can be played anywhere—Archimedes did it in a bathtub.
—Richard J. Trudeau

INTRODUCTION TO MATH CENTERS AND AGENDAS

Math and centers? Yes! This is a wonderful way to engage students in meaningful and authentic learning. Beyond elementary school? Sure! Students gain much from what centers bring to a classroom. As Trudeau states above, educators have an opportunity to engage our students in the "world's best game" that won't cost them a dime and is easy to do in a variety of ways and locations. With the kinesthetic movement and variety of instruction available in the use of centers, the teacher meet students' needs through this differentiation tactic. Math manipulatives can provide that connection to learning that many students miss in their formative training on concepts. For instance, rather than a whole-class lesson of direct instruction on how to do the algorithm of long division, students can use inquiry methods to discover mathematics in a more meaningful way.

Through math centers, students have the opportunity to work on many skills. Some of those can be knowing and using numbers; investigating and solving problems; using practical skills of estimation, measurement, and accuracy; using technology applications; demonstrating variables and patterns; using tables and graphs; using algebra; demonstrating geometric understanding; constructing proofs; making predictions and formulating questions; and collecting data to analyze and communicate results. Centers allow for the format of discovery rather than rote memorization.

Teachers and students gain much from the use of centers in the math classroom. Centers provide a format and environment for enhancing arithmetic skills and creative problem solving. The tasks are to be educational and engaging at the same time. Centers should align with the curriculum and support the work that is being done at that time in the classroom. The tasks should be more than worksheets or textbook problems, but rather hands-on and minds-on activities to deepen understanding (Dodrill, 2011).

The math centers should be connected to the curriculum and work that is being done in the classroom. The centers provide opportunity to get at readiness/process, interest/content, and learning preference/product. The teacher can approach a student at his readiness level by providing practice with a process in which he needs deeper understanding. For example, "Making Ten" might be a process center at the primary level. Teachers can use centers to appeal to the interest of the child through a certain aspect of math content. For example, the student may write a math story for a concept she is learning about during that time. The learning styles can be spotlighted and encouraged through product choice. For example, the student may be given a Think-Tac-Toe with choices given to emphasize problem-solving explanations and processes, but with a choice of nine different products.

An important correlation to remember with this chapter is that the centers are aligned to the grade-level standards. Oftentimes in mathematics, if a child is working above grade level on the standards, the teacher may choose to single-subject accelerate the student to the next grade level (Assouline & Lupkowski-Shoplik, 2005). Keep in mind, however, that accelerating to the next grade level does not mean that differentiation is no longer needed. Even within an accelerated design, differentiation should always be at the forefront of planning in every scenario for planning instruction.

Discussion of Standards

The Common Core Mathematics Standards should be considered when designing the centers and agendas for your classroom (Common Core State Standards Initiative, 2011a). At the kindergarten level, the standards are Counting and Cardinality; Operations and Algebraic Thinking; Number and Operations in Base 10; Geometry; and Measurement and Data. Grades 1–2 continue with all of the standards from kindergarten with the exception of Counting and Cardinality. Grades 3–5 continue with all grades 1–2 standards and add Number and Operations of Fractions. Grades 6–7 transition away from Operations and Algebraic Thinking, Number and Operations, and Measurement and Data toward Ratios and Proportional Relationships, The Number System, Expressions and Equations, and Statistics and Probability. Grade 8 transitions away from Ratios and Proportional Relationships and The Number System to add Functions. The Common Core Standards are the following:

- Counting and Cardinality (K)

- Operations and Algebraic Thinking (K–5)
- Expressions and Equations (6–8)
- Number and Operations in Base Ten (K–5)
- Number and Operations of Fractions (3–5)
- Ratios and Proportional Relationships (6–7)
- The Number System (6–8)
- Functions (8)
- Geometry (K–8)
- Measurement and Data (K–5)
- Statistics and Probability (6–8). (Common Core State Standards Initiative, 2011a)

Included along with the content standards, the Standards for Mathematical Practice (Common Core State Standards Initiative, 2011b) should also be considered in the rationale behind why teachers of mathematics can use centers and agendas to effectively meet the needs of students. As seen below, if a student is to "make sense of problems and persevere in solving them," what better way to do this than through a center? It is difficult in a traditional classroom with a traditional format to allow for the time it takes for a student to persevere to solve a rigorous problem-solving task. The mathematical practices encompass a sense of inquiry that can be met through centers.

Standards for Mathematical Practice
- Make sense of problems and persevere in solving them.
- Reason abstractly and quantitatively.
- Construct viable arguments and critique the reasoning of others.
- Model with mathematics.
- Use appropriate tools strategically.
- Attend to precision.
- Look for and make use of structure.
- Look for and express regularity in repeated reasoning. (Common Core State Standards Initiative, 2011b)

DIFFERENTIATION OF CONTENT VIA INTERESTS

Content differentiation can be handled by differentiation of interests. This is one of the easiest and quickest ways to differentiate content when coupling it with interest. However, it is important to keep the content at the forefront every step of the way as to ensure that the interest aspect does not overtake the learning of the content. To do this, be very intentional in expectations for how to have the student exhibit his or her learning.

The following set of centers is based on student interest. For teachers to see how centers can be organized by content through interests, the inclusive standard of Number and Operations and the Number System is explored through a scaffolded example of centers given. These, at *all* levels, would be set up at different areas of the room and would have small groups at each. The centers are named the same, intentionally, at each grade band level to show how the scaffolding can progress when applied to different grade levels.

Multiple Student Interest Centers (Grades K–2)

Standard Addressed: Common Core Standard: Number and Operations in Base 10.

Shopping Spree: Using selected online stores, mail-order, or old store catalogs and advertisements, have students peruse the resources and provide a fun way for students to explore what they would be interested in purchasing. This learning experience becomes an educational math center when students determine the items they want to purchase given a certain amount of money. Students are required to show their purchases and totals. To connect to their interests, students have the same content but it is varied by what shopping they choose to do (Frost, 2011).

Classroom Store: Set up a store to help students practice buying and selling items. Students at this center assume roles of shopkeeper, supervisor, and customers. Money and a cash register should be provided, as well as items for them to "purchase."

Computation War: Students use a deck of cards to work on adding numbers. The teacher may choose to remove certain cards from the deck to limit or focus on certain computations to be performed. Pairs or groups of students play this together like the traditional "War" card game, but with a twist. Each round, students flip over two cards and add the two cards together. The winning student for the round is the one with the highest sum. If there is a tie, students flip over two more cards and go through the process again. The person with the highest sum earns all of the cards for the round. Variations for this include three cards for addends. Another variation is subtracting the smaller number from the larger number of the pair.

Captain's Coming—Compute!: In a group of three with a deck of cards, one student is the captain who gives the other two student soldiers a card from the deck. When the captain says, "Compute!", student soldiers hold their card face out on their forehead as a salute to the captain. The captain provides the sum and each soldier guesses their addend/card that they cannot see by using the clue of the other soldier's card. To increase the rigor, increase the number of soldiers.

Can You Catch It?: Use a beach ball and write numbers all over the surface. One at a time, have a student announce a classmate's name and roll the ball to that person in the small group. The catcher adds the number that the left thumb lands on to the number that the roller says before rolling the ball. Continue this cycle again.

Multiple Student Interest Centers (Grades 3–5)

Standard Addressed: Common Core Standard: Number and Operations in Base 10.

Shopping Spree: Given a set amount of money, students shop on approved online sites and in catalogs and develop a list of their expenditures. They need to compute the sales tax to get the grand total. Students create an expenditure report for their purchases. They present their findings and purchases using technology, displaying the growing total throughout. They also discuss the impact of taxes on the total (Frost, 2011). A possible extension could be to have a debate about taxes including topics such as the fairness of taxes and/or why some items are taxed and others are not.

Classroom Store: Set up a kiosk to help students practice buying and selling items, including tax. Students at this center assume roles of cashier, owner, and customers. Money and a cash register should be provided, as well as items for them to "purchase." An end-of-week report to the stockholders should be provided each week, giving a record of the sales. Students should generate questions and scenarios about working at a kiosk such as what could go wrong while at work and how to overcome the scenario in a positive manner.

Computation War: This game works on skills of multiplication and more. With a deck of cards, pairs or groups of students play this together like the traditional "War" card game, but with a twist. Each round, students flip over two cards and multiply the two cards together. The winning student for the round is the one with the highest product. If there is a tie, students flip over two more cards and go through the process again. The person with the highest product earns all of the cards for the round. Variations for this include three cards to multiply for the product. Another variation is where the larger number is the denominator and the lower number is the numerator—the fraction with the highest value wins. Students can write problem-solving scenarios using the cards as the numbers to be included in the scenarios.

Captain's Coming—Compute!: In a group of three with a deck of cards, one student is the captain who gives the two student soldiers a card from the deck. When the captain says, "Compute!", student soldiers hold their card face out on their forehead as a salute to the captain. The captain provides the product and each soldier gives the value of the card that they cannot see from the clue of the other soldier's card. To increase the rigor, increase the number of soldiers and cards per round.

Can You Catch It?: Write numbers with operations on a beach ball. For example, one might be "multiply by 6." Have a student in the group say a number and a person's name to catch the ball, then throw the ball to that person in the small group. The catcher uses the stated number and the operation that the student's left thumb touches to create an answer. Focus on the skills of multiplication and division.

Multiple Student Interest Centers (Grades 6–8)

Standard Addressed: Common Core Standard: The Number System.

Shopping Spree: Assuming the role of a Personal Shopper, have students pretend they have $1 million to spend for a person. Have them choose a client to partner with and interview—possibly a teacher, peer, or family member that they are representing to find out the needs and wants for the purchases. Students will then have the freedom to choose the items for purchase. They should calculate taxes and also plan for what may need to be insured or what may have a reoccurring expense. Students will then present a purchasing portfolio for their chosen client. The portfolio may be created using Prezi (Calhoon, 2011) or other presentation tools.

Classroom Store: Students set up an online store and construct a website to learn how to deal with all aspects of sales: supply/inventory, advertising, coupons, and short-term sales. Students at this center assume roles of webmaster, owner, and customers. The students decide as a small group or class as to what items will be available for them to "purchase." An end-of-week report to the stockholders should be provided each week giving a record of the sales. They will also need to develop a plan for increasing sales.

Computation War: Students use a deck of cards to work on multiplying positive and negative integers. The red cards are negative numbers and the black cards are positive numbers. Two or more cards are drawn at a time and multiplied together. Each round, students flip over two cards and multiply the two cards together. The winning student for the round is the one with the highest product. If there is a tie, students flip over two more cards and go through the process again. The person with the highest product earns all of the cards for the round. Variations for this include three cards to multiply for the product. Students can write problem-solving scenarios using the cards as the numbers to be included in the scenarios.

Captain's Coming—Compute!: In a group of four with a deck of cards, one student is the captain who gives the three student soldiers a card from the deck. When the captain says, "Compute!", student soldiers hold their card face out on their forehead as a salute to the captain. The captain provides the sum or the product and each soldier gives the value of the card that they cannot see from the clue of the other soldiers' cards. A red card is negative and a black card is positive, giving practice with sums or products of positive and negative numbers.

Can You Catch It?: Write equations on a beach ball. The format of the equations needs to have a variable to solve for and a position for a constant announced to be place. For example, with $2x + n = 10$, the student would plug in the announced number into the "n" position and solve for "x." Have a student announce a classmate's name and announce a number. The student throws the ball to that person. The catcher plugs in the announced number for "n" and solves for "x." The catcher becomes the pitcher and announces a new number and name and throws. A variation could be to have the students take these equations and create a problem that would match.

DIFFERENTIATION OF PROCESS VIA ABILITY AND READINESS LEVEL

Try differentiating the process through ability and readiness level. This approach can provide the most focused instruction and aligns well with Response to Intervention philosophy. Due to the fact that gifted children's educational needs differ from other children with regard to pace and complexity (Daniel & Cox, 1988; Kaplan, 2007; Maker, 1982; Parke, 1992), this gives these children an opportunity to achieve at a more rigorous cognitive level (Gavin, Casa, Adelson, Carroll, & Sheffield, 2009). With this differentiation design, everyone can be studying the same content topic at the same time, yet some will experience and learn on different levels than others. The levels for the examples are shown for beginning, practicing, and stretching. By pre-assessing the students over the content, it is possible to plan and focus on meeting children's needs.

The leveled centers that follow should be run simultaneously in the classroom. The design for this may vary when incorporating the different levels of students and determining how to do the rotations. However, consider dividing the room into the three opportunity/level areas. One way to do this is for the teacher to work with the beginning group, while the practicing and stretching group work independently. Or, the teacher may have all groups working in the levels, circulating and facilitating, while using a checklist to note skills observed. If any one level is too large to be one group, split those students into more than one group.

Mind Your Measurement (Grades K–2)

Standard Addressed: Common Core Standard: First Grade Measurement and Data.

Beginning: Provide a laminated sheet with three objects drawn on it. Have students measure all of the objects using a paperclip. They should then answer the question, "How many paper clip lengths does it take to find each object length?" Students should record their findings in a chart and create a bar graph.

Practicing: Provide three different objects of three varying lengths. Have students measure the lengths of the two objects using the third and shortest object. They should then use a Mathematician Observation Journal to record their findings. They should then answer the questions, "Which is the longer of the two? What are other observations you can make from this activity? Choose three other objects to measure. How do these compare?" Finally, students should give a presentation about their findings.

Stretching: Using two different objects for measurement, students should make a prediction about how many of each of the measurement objects it will take to measure three different items of their choice. Have students organize their data into a chart, then write an acceptance speech for winning the First-Grade Measurement Prize that highlights their findings.

Mind Your Measurement (Grades 3–5)

Standard Addressed: Common Core Standard: Fourth-Grade Measurement and Data.

Beginning: Students will recognize angles as geometric shapes that are formed wherever two rays share a common endpoint. They should model with a partner how to show rays by acting them out and taking digital photos to document their ideas. As an extension, they can find or take digital pictures with a variety of angles and determine the type of angles they find, then classify them into categories. Finally, students can use the digital photos from the first two parts to create an Animoto to highlight their findings.

Practicing: Students should explain the relationship between a ray and an angle. They should write a script with at least two characters—a ray and an angle. The characters' identities should clearly come out during the play through their words and actions. Students may choose to also include the role of the circle. Then have students draw 10 angles of their choice, measure each of them to the nearest degree, and display their work on a poster.

Stretching: Students will create a visual art display of a ray—more than one may be in the artwork. Then they will write an accompanying autobiography of a ray to discuss the trials and successes of being a ray. After this, they should define an angle and answer these questions: "How are rays used to find the measurement? What is the role of the circle in finding angle measurement?" Have students make a video answering these questions and their own questions, and then explain how to measure an angle with a tool of their choice (e.g., protractor).

Mind Your Measurement (Grades 6–8)

Standard Addressed: Common Core Standard: Sixth-Grade Ratios and Proportional Relationships.

Beginning: Provide two baskets to draw a slip of paper from at this center. Have one basket with items to measure and the other basket providing the scale ratio. Have students use a proportion to solve the missing dimensions for the drawing, as in this example:

> If you select a picture of a wading pool that measures 6 ft by 10 ft and select a scale that is 1 cm to 2 ft, picture to actual, what would the dimensions for the scale object be? The 6 ft would be 3 cm and the 10 ft would be 5 cm.
>
> 1 cm / 2 ft = x cm / 6 ft
>
> x = 3 ft

Through the role of tutor, students can present their findings in a PhotoPeach presentation with questions developed from the slips they drew from the baskets (Sanders, 2011).

Practicing: Give students this scenario: "You are the principal of the school and need to tell teachers the measurements of the school. Given a blueprint of the school, find the actual measurements using the ratio provided on the drawing." (Students are provided with a school blueprint that gives the scale for the measurements represented on the drawing—the actual measurements are not included.) Students should then find the measurements of places of their choice to be able to share with their teachers and classmates. They must design a couple of choices for an addition to the school that addresses a need that they believe is important for them and their classmates. Then, they must set up a debate about the need for one of these additions and incorporate how the dimensions were calculated from the blueprint scale.

Stretching: Give students this scenario: "The floor plan for the school has been lost. Many people visit your school because of its wonderful students and teachers. You are the chairperson for the welcoming committee to help make sure people know the dimensions to certain areas of the school given the accurate floor plan." Have students measure a portion of the school. Provide paper and supplies for them to draw a floor plan of the location. They should determine the scale used for their drawing and show how this scale is accurately reflected in the drawing. Then, have students write a speech to give to the school board and their parents that discusses how they believe the accuracy of the floor plan can be trusted and any improvements to the school that might be considered. Students can design a Prezi to accompany their speech that displays their accuracy and thinking process in coming up with the floor plan.

DIFFERENTIATION OF PRODUCT VIA LEARNING STYLE

Differentiation based on learning style can be accomplished through choice in product. Although many styles can be tapped for the design, one way is to look at the products promoted in Roberts and Inman's (2009b) work. They share that products may be technological (e.g., blogs, web pages, PowerPoint presentations), visual (e.g., posters, pamphlets, drawings), written (e.g., essays, vignettes, articles), oral (e.g., speeches, interviews, monologues), or kinesthetic (e.g., models, dioramas, role play). To help in scoring the variety of products that are potentially submitted in this design, use the DAP Tool for guiding the students in targeting quality products and in assisting with scoring (Roberts & Inman, 2009a). The following three examples (see Figure 6.1, Figure 6.2, and Figure 6.3) are based on the multiple intelligences as explored in Gardner's (1983) *Frames of Mind: The Theory of Multiple Intelligences*.

PUTTING IT ALL TOGETHER: CONTENT, PROCESS, AND PRODUCT DIFFERENTIATION

Throughout this chapter, you have seen a variety of ways to differentiate based on content, process, or product. This section will now provide you with a single-grade range differentiated on a single topic to help give another angle for considering how differentiation can be designed and understood. The following set of centers shows how one standard, fractions, can be applied in all three formats of differentiated centers. This applies to a third-grade standard, but could easily be adapted and designed to work for any grade level with any standard.

The design of this example set could be used as a growing set of centers or as stand-alone centers. Depending on the amount of time and depth preferred in the product, this may take up to 2 weeks to complete one to all of these products. One way to consider this is that content is Phase 1, process is Phase 2, and product is Phase 3. The preassessment (see Figure 6.4) provides a possible design for how to

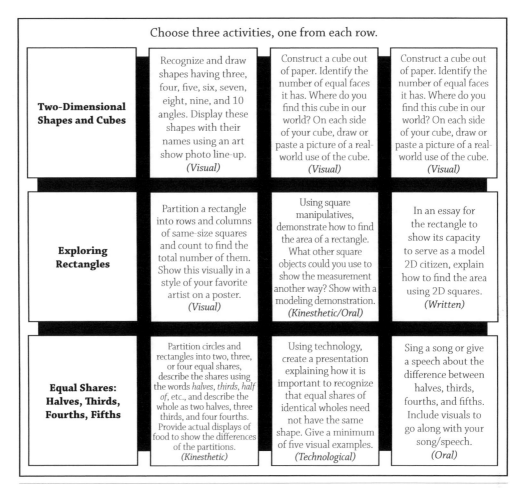

Figure 6.1. Geometry Think-Tac-Toe, grades K–2.

consider the approach to assessing content, process, and product variables prior to the instruction.

Math Book (Grades 3–5): Content Via Interests

Standard Addressed: Common Core Standard: Third-Grade Number and Operations—Fractions.

Teacher Preparation: Provide supplies for students to have access to materials to create a book. This may entail computer/printer availability, paper, scissors, stapler, yarn, construction paper, glue, and magazines, among other supplies, for a book-making location.

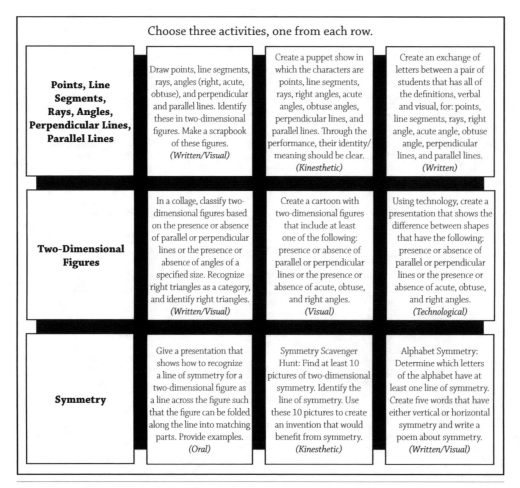

Figure 6.2. Geometry Think-Tac-Toe, grades 3–5.

Student Instructions: Choose a topic that you are interested in—like dinosaurs, video games, hiking, and so forth. Write a math book to show your understanding of equivalent fractions. Include an explanation as to why whole numbers are fractions and what they are equivalent to as well. Also, explain how you know when one fraction is larger than another.

Wacky Word Problems (Grades 3–5): Process Via Ability and Readiness

Standard Addressed: Common Core Standard: Third-Grade Number and Operations—Fractions.

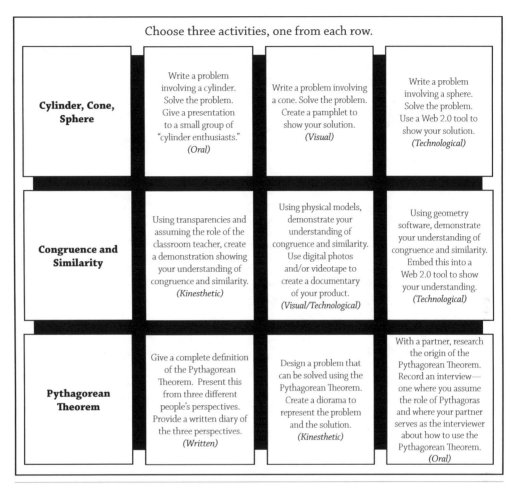

Choose three activities, one from each row.			
Cylinder, Cone, Sphere	Write a problem involving a cylinder. Solve the problem. Give a presentation to a small group of "cylinder enthusiasts." *(Oral)*	Write a problem involving a cone. Solve the problem. Create a pamphlet to show your solution. *(Visual)*	Write a problem involving a sphere. Solve the problem. Use a Web 2.0 tool to show your solution. *(Technological)*
Congruence and Similarity	Using transparencies and assuming the role of the classroom teacher, create a demonstration showing your understanding of congruence and similarity. *(Kinesthetic)*	Using physical models, demonstrate your understanding of congruence and similarity. Use digital photos and/or videotape to create a documentary of your product. *(Visual/Technological)*	Using geometry software, demonstrate your understanding of congruence and similarity. Embed this into a Web 2.0 tool to show your understanding. *(Technological)*
Pythagorean Theorem	Give a complete definition of the Pythagorean Theorem. Present this from three different people's perspectives. Provide a written diary of the three perspectives. *(Written)*	Design a problem that can be solved using the Pythagorean Theorem. Create a diorama to represent the problem and the solution. *(Kinesthetic)*	With a partner, research the origin of the Pythagorean Theorem. Record an interview—one where you assume the role of Pythagoras and where your partner serves as the interviewer about how to use the Pythagorean Theorem. *(Oral)*

Figure 6.3. Geometry Think-Tac-Toe, grades 6–8.

Teacher Preparation: Find several pictures and words in magazines, cut them out, and make two separate envelopes—one for the words and one for the pictures. Provide construction paper, glue, and markers as well.

Beginning, Student Instructions: Using two different envelopes, choose a student representative in your small group to randomly select a magazine picture from one envelope and a magazine word from a second envelope. You will write a "Wacky Word Problem" incorporating this picture and word into a mathematics word problem that requires an equivalent fraction for the solution. Your product will be to construct a magazine page for the "Wacky Word Problem" section. Be sure to include a solution section.

Practicing, Student Instructions: Using two different envelopes, choose a representative in your small group to randomly select two magazine pictures from one envelope

Content via Interests:
1. What topics are you interested in that involve thinking in portions?
2. How can you show your understanding of fractions with this interest?

Process via Ability and Readiness (if students master all four, ready for "Stretching" portion and if 3 of 4 correct, ready for "Practicing" portion.):
3. On the back of the paper, define "fraction" then explain a fraction in reference to what you already know about mathematics. Be sure to give examples to support the answer.
4. On the back of the paper, draw a picture that displays your understanding of fractions.
5. On the back of the paper, give an example of why fractions are important to understand.
6. On the back of the paper, write a math problem that involves fractions.

Product via Learning Style:
7. Circle those products that you have created before.
8. Put a star beside those products that interest you that you have not created before.

Diorama	Mask	Model	Sculpture
Debate	Interview	Monologue	Oral Presentation
Computer Graphic	Movie	Podcast	PowerPoint
Cartoon	Collage	Pamphlet	Poster
Diary	Essay	Letter	Written Interview

Figure 6.4. Fractions preassessment.

and two magazine words from a second envelope. You will write a "Wacky Word Problem" incorporating the pictures and words into two problems that requires a comparison of fractions for the solution. The problems must be significantly different from one another. Students provide a solution/answer key to the problem. Your product will be to construct a Glogster page that displays the two problems and solutions.

Stretching, Student Instructions: Using two different envelopes, choose a student representative from your small group to randomly select two magazine pictures from one envelope and two magazine words from a second envelope. Students will write a "Wacky Word Problem" incorporating the pictures and words into a two-part problem. The first part requires a comparison of fractions by using the denominator; and the second part, by looking at the numerator. Provide a solution/answer key that includes a visual model. Design a Blabberize or Xtranormal presentation to present your problem parts and how your group designed and thought through the process.

Fractions—What Portions Do We Know? (Grades 3–5): Product Via Learning Style

This center is designed around the learning styles of: Mastery, Understanding, Self-Expressive, and Interpersonal (Silver, Strong, & Perini, 2000). This set of learning styles helps teachers cope with the individual differences. The learning types are:

- Mastery Style (Sensing-Thinking)
  - Sensitivity to acts, details, physical actions, steps
  - Inclination for remembering, describing, manipulating, ordering
  - Ability to organize, report, build, plan, and execute projects

- Understanding Style (Intuitive-Thinking)
  - Sensitivity to gaps/flaws, questions, patterns, ideas
  - Inclination for analyzing, testing/proving, examining, connecting
  - Ability to argue, research, develop theories, explain

- Self-Expressive Style (Intuitive-Feeling)
  - Sensitivity to hunches, images, possibilities, inspiration
  - Inclination for predicting/speculating, imagining, generating ideas, developing insights
  - Ability to develop original solutions, think metaphorically, articulate ideas, express, and create

- Interpersonal Style (Sensing-Feeling)
  - Sensitivity to feelings, people, gut reactions, experiences
  - Inclination for supporting, personalizing, expressing emotions, experiential learning
  - Ability to build trust and rapport, empathize, respond, teach

Mastery, Student Instructions: Write an online step-by-step manual (e.g., using a WordPress blog) or create an online poster (e.g., on Glogster) for how to find equivalent fractions and how to compare fractions. Design and incorporate a plan for how to explain this to those younger than you or to struggling classmates.

Understanding, Student Instructions: Look through your math book and computer resources to find what information is provided for equivalent fractions and how to compare fractions. Analyze and synthesize what you find in all of these resources to provide one pamphlet that could be given to parents and classmates to help them understand more about fractions.

Self-Expressive, Student Instructions: Using technology presentation software (e.g., Xtranormal) or by creating a piece of art, depict an explanation that shows your understanding of equivalent fractions and comparison of fractions. Give the explanation for both from three different points of view—your choice.

Interpersonal, Student Instructions: With a small group, prepare a skit where you role-play to show your understanding of equivalent fractions and how to compare fractions. Be sure to include vocabulary that is key to understanding the instruction through the skit.

CONCLUSION

"Doing math" means more than memorizing facts and applying algorithms for computation. "Doing math" is where students are applying their knowledge, creating connections, and analyzing solutions to complex problems. Through math centers, students can learn math and work at their individual ability levels at their own speed. The focus can be on accuracy and the process rather than the answer. Students are motivated and build self-confidence while enjoying the nonroutine format for learning. Most importantly, students learn that math is a process and not simply memorization. The purpose of centers is for students to see real-world math in action (Math Lessons, 2011).

An overarching technique that I recently heard Dr. Carol Ann Tomlinson (2011) share was: "Give students the problem and the answer—the task is find three ways to work the problem." To me, this is the epitome of learning math at any time, and it also pushes into higher levels of thinking.

CHAPTER 6 RESOURCES

Animoto—http://www.animoto.com
Ask Dr. Math—http://mathforum.org/dr.math
Blabberize—http:// blabberize.com
Fresh Baked Fractions—http://www.funbrain.com/fract/index.html
Glogster—http://www.glogster.com
Math Buddy—http://www.mathbuddyonline.com
Math Centers—http://lessonplanz.com/Lesson_Plans/Learning_Centers/Math_
    Centers/index.shtml
Math Centers (Part I)—http://teachers.net/lessons/posts/549.html
Math Centres—http://www.canteach.ca/elementary/mathcentres.html
Math Classroom Resources—http://www.pbs.org/teachers/classroom/k-2/math/
    resources
Math Instructional Ideas—http://www.littlegiraffes.com/math.html

Math Playground—http://www.mathplayground.com
PBS Teachers—http://www.pbs.org/teachers
PhotoPeach—http://www.photopeach.com
Preschool–Kindergarten Lesson Plans for Meeting the Curriculum—http://www.
kinderplans.com/PreschoolKindergartenLessons
Prezi—http://www.prezi.com
Scholastic Teachers—http://www2.scholastic.com/browse/teach.jsp
Teacher2Teacher—http://mathforum.org/t2t
WordPress—http://www.wordpress.org
Xtranormal—http://www.xtranormal.com
LessonPlanZ.com—http://lessonplanz.com
Kingore, B. (2011). *Tiered learning stations in minutes! Increasing achievement, high-level thinking, and the joy of learning.* Austin, TX: Professional Associates.
Ronis, D. (2001). *Brain-compatible mathematics.* Thousand Oaks, CA: Corwin Press.

REFERENCES

Assouline, S., & Lupkowski-Shoplik, A. (2005). *Developing math talent: A guide for educating gifted and advanced learners in math.* Waco, TX: Prufrock Press.
Calhoon, B. (2011). *Math center ideas for middle school.* Retrieved from http://www.ehow.com/info_7868557_math-center-ideas-middle-school.html#ixzz1EvqUgq13
Common Core State Standards Initiative. (2011a). *Mathematics standards.* Retrieved from http://www.corestandards.org/the-standards/mathematics
Common Core State Standards Initiative. (2011b). *Standards for mathematical practice.* Retrieved from http://www.corestandards.org/the-standards/mathematics/introduction/standards-for-mathematical-practice/
Daniel, N., & Cox, J. (1988). *Flexible pacing for able learners.* Reston, VA: Council for Exceptional Children.
Dodrill, T. (2011). *About math centers in the classroom.* Retrieved from http://www.ehow.com/info_7862456_math-centers-classroom.html#ixzz1EvNZlYSu
Frost, S. (2011). *Learning center ideas for math.* Retrieved from http://www.ehow.com/way_5208692_learning-center-ideas-math.html#ixzz1EvLh0Mfu
Gardner, H. (1983). *Frames of mind: The theory of multiple intelligences.* New York, NY: Basic Books.
Gavin, M. K., Casa, T. M., Adelson, J. L., Carroll, S. R., & Sheffield, L. J. (2009). The impact of advanced curriculum on the achievement of mathematically promising elementary students. *Gifted Child Quarterly, 53,* 188–202.
Kaplan, S. (2007). Differentiation by depth and complexity. In W. Conklin & S. Frei (Eds.), *Differentiating the curriculum for gifted learners* (pp. 79–88). Huntington Beach, CA: Shell Education.

Maker, J. (1982). *Curriculum development for the gifted.* Rockville, MD: Aspen Systems.

Math Lessons. (2011). *Math learning center.* Retrieved from http://www.math-lessons.ca/blog/2007/11/14/math-learning-center

Parke, B. N. (1992). *Challenging gifted students in the regular classroom.* Retrieved from http://www.nagc.org/index.aspx?id=143

Roberts, J. L., & Inman, T. F. (2009a). *Assessing differentiated student products: A protocol for development and evaluation.* Waco, TX: Prufrock Press.

Roberts, J. L., & Inman, T. F. (2009b). *Strategies for differentiating instruction: Best practices for the classroom* (2nd ed.). Waco, TX: Prufrock Press.

Sanders, A. (2011). *Fifth grade math center activities.* Retrieved from http://www.ehow.com/info_7882451_fifth-grade-math-center-activities.html#ixzz1EvRKLFK2

Silver, H. F., Strong, R. W., & Perini, M. J. (2000). *So each may learn: Integrating learning styles and multiple intelligences.* Alexandria, VA: Association for Supervision and Curriculum Development.

Tomlinson, C. A. (2011). *Differentiating instruction: 6 guidelines & some tools.* Presentation for Wedge Visiting Professor Series, Western Kentucky University, Bowling Green, KY.

Differentiation in Visual and Performing Arts:
Using Multidisciplinary Agendas and Centers to Foster Continuous Progress

Jan W. Lanham

The task of art is enormous. Through the influence of real art, aided by science, guided by religion, that peaceful co-operation of man is now obtained by external means—by law courts, police, charitable institutions, factory inspection, etc.—should be obtained by man's free and joyous activity. Art should cause violence to be set aside. And it is only art that can accomplish this. All human life is filled with works of art of every kind—from cradlesong, jest, mimicry, the ornamentation of houses, dress, and utensils, up to church services, buildings, monuments, and triumphal processions. It is all artistic activity.

—Leo Tolstoy

Tolstoy vividly expressed the vital role of the arts in daily life. Recognizing that importance, educators strive to integrate the arts into every content area, while nurturing students who possess unique artistic talents. The process of designing multidisciplinary and diagnostic arts differentiation presents unique challenges. It is important to provide basic arts experiences for all students while providing direct instruction that assures continuous progress for those students who demonstrate advanced ability in one or more arts disciplines.

Although most teachers enjoy the variety of products and processes that emerge as arts concepts are integrated in the classroom, lack of expertise may cause many classroom teachers to lose confidence when designing and assessing quality arts-based products. That expertise gap is heightened when asked to select content or processes and to assess products for students who seem to demonstrate advanced proficiency in one or more arts disciplines. Matching instructional opportunities in the arts based on student interests, needs, and abilities can be particularly daunting within the context of content-based instruction.

The Common Core State Standards (National Governors Association & Council of Chief State School Officers, 2010), adopted by most states, acknowledge the importance of arts integration as evidenced by the wealth of arts activities included in the Common Core State Standards curriculum maps found at http://commoncore.org/maps. The use of real-world products and interdisciplinary connections within those documents and in state-level documents lays the groundwork for including a common set of arts experiences for all students. By incorporating quality unit design and high-level expectations of daily attention to multiple modalities for process and product, the foundation for differentiation through centers and agendas can be expanded.

A variety of artistic products should be included in multidisciplinary differentiation. They provide a full range of modalities through which students are able to demonstrate mastery of concepts in all content areas at a variety of levels. As centers and agendas are developed, it is imperative to include differentiated content, processes, and products based in visual and performing arts in order to provide choices and real-world connections that foster creative problem solving and synthesis of complex understandings. Although arts products as a choice for all students are important, differentiation for students with high potential in the arts must be diagnostically designed to reflect experiences and training that target student growth in their strength areas. This chapter will address both levels of differentiation in the arts—differentiation through arts integration and differentiation to foster continuous progress in the arts.

USING MULTIDISCIPLINARY DIFFERENTIATION TO FOSTER CONTINUOUS PROGRESS IN VISUAL AND PERFORMING ARTS

All students benefit from the opportunity to create and perform through multiple modalities, while students identified with advanced skills in one or more arts disciplines require specific training to assure continuous progress in those areas. That specific training is vital to establish the context inherent in the college and career readiness facets of the Common Core Standards. The differences in purpose and intentionality for different students have the potential to create an instructional gap. Integration of arts processes and products in the regular classroom with quality rubrics and an emphasis on self-assessment are keys to assuring continuous progress in arts instruction. This process requires accurately preassessing student levels of readiness and mastery, accessing the appropriate standards, and teaming with building-level professionals with the expertise to strengthen classroom activities and assessments in the arts.

Planning for and implementing the arts may appear daunting, as there are students with gifts and talents in each of the arts disciplines, and there are myriad standards within each of those disciplines. It is important for classroom teachers to remember that there are resources available to provide support and that there are individuals with specific areas of expertise who can lend support in the process of integrating that instruction across all content areas.

In addition to fostering connections with experts who can enhance instruction for all students, the process of using multidisciplinary centers and agendas has a genuine efficiency benefit. As students work on a variety of high-level tasks built around common standards and learning targets, they gain increased expertise about their specific areas of study. When students share their products and go through the process of peer and self-reflection, all students benefit from hearing and seeing other students' products and findings. Differentiated peer products are usually produced at a depth that would not be possible with whole-group coverage of those same concepts. In addition, the ongoing work with assessment criteria helps students internalize those standards, making multidisciplinary agendas and centers a foundation for strong instruction.

DIFFERENTIATING WITH A MULTIDISCIPLINARY AGENDA

A typical multidisciplinary agenda will include opportunities for students to choose content, processes, and products that address varied modalities. Students may choose to present their findings in written form, in a song, as a poster series, as a cartoon series, and so forth. Although the products are assessed with a rubric linked to the specific elements of the product, the indicators are generic and link the research, reading, writing, or thinking skill to product effectiveness.

Multidisciplinary differentiation typically provides increased opportunity for student choice and opportunity for the teacher to target specific growth areas matched to student needs, while working from a common set of standards and learning targets. All students benefit from product differentiation that allows them to address interests and learning styles. Students who have demonstrated mastery of targeted arts skills, concepts, or content will require additional differentiation to assure continuous progress.

Reading

Standards Addressed: ELA.CCR10: Read and comprehend literary and informational texts independently and proficiently; ELA.CCW4.7: Conduct short research projects that build knowledge through investigation of different aspects of a topic.

A fundamental goal for all students is the ELA.CCR10 standard. This standard is repeatedly addressed at all grade levels and provides opportunities for differentiation through content, process, and product.

When paired with the ELA.CCW4.7 standard, an agenda and differentiated stations can readily be developed. Because these standards scaffold in depth and complexity, they can be easily modified up or down for different grade levels and different student needs.

Learning Target: Students will demonstrate understanding of the events and feelings of individuals involved in desegregation and make connections to their personal experiences.

Lesson Hook: "What would it be like to feel that you didn't belong or you didn't fit in? How does the behavior of adults influence how you feel and how you act?"

Assignment: Students read *The Story of Ruby Bridges* by Robert Coles (1995) and participate in a discussion of the book. They select additional activities from the Think-Tac-Toe (see Figure 7.1) to link reading, research, and presentation skills. Each activity can be made more or less complex according to student readiness and needs, but each provides a basic opportunity for high-level thinking and student application of the content and skills in a multidisciplinary format.

Assessment: Each task will be scored by a rubric that reflects the general and specific criteria for success. Rubrics can be adjusted to reflect differentiated requirements that show continuous progress. As students in the class prepare and present varied products, all students benefit. By providing peer assessment of the products they see and hear, they internalize mastery criteria for different tasks and they gain exposure to content explored by their peers.

Each of the Think-Tac-Toe activities could be reformatted to represent learning centers with appropriate resources and product materials available. Each product has a visual or performing arts link that should be specifically addressed with appropriate skill training and resources based on student needs. Progress toward those skills is specifically addressed in rubrics that identify mastery criteria.

Writing (Focus on Research)

Standards Addressed: National Science Education Standards (NSES; National Research Council, 1996) Life Science C at the Elementary Level: Students should develop understanding of the characteristics of organisms, life cycles of organisms, and organisms and environments; ELA4.9: Draw evidence from literary or information texts to support analysis, reflection, and research to provide multidisciplinary centers for differentiation.

By combining the NSES Life Science C standard with the writing standard ELA4.9, several centers are easily developed. Although the initial plan for these standards

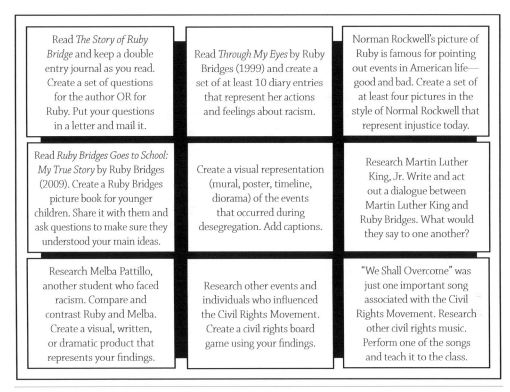

Figure 7.1. *The Story of Ruby Bridges* Think-Tac-Toe.

was built around fourth-grade students, as the activities and extensions are explored, they are readily adapted for younger or older students.

Center 1: Ecosystems

Assignment: Create a world map that illustrates at least four different ecosystems. Include the habitats, organisms, interrelationships, climate, and threats to each ecosystem. Use flip pages on the map to provide "layers" of information that reflect changes over time, predator-prey and food chain links, and possible solutions to the problems facing the ecosystem.

Arts Differentiation, Student Instructions: The arts differentiation options could be made available to all students as extensions addressing varied learning styles. For students identified in an area of visual/performing arts, however, it is important that the assignment of those extensions is diagnostic and that the teacher provides support, instruction, and resources that help talented arts students make continuous progress on targeted skills. As multidisciplinary differentiation, the extension task is usually in addition to the basic task unless the student is able to demonstrate the content understanding in another way.

- *Music:* Choose one of your ecosystems. Create and produce a commercial jingle integrating the key attributes of your ecosystem in music.
- *Drama*: Assume the role of a travel agent or inhabitant of one of your ecosystems. Write and present a monologue as that character to convince others of the wonders of your location.
- *Visual Art:* Create a cartoon series that represents one of your ecosystems from the point of view of the plant and animal life. Be sure your captions are fact-filled. Incorporate humor and irony as possible.
- *Dance:* Research the music/dance of one of your geographic areas. Use that dance style to create a dance that uses movement to tell others about one ecosystem, its inhabitants, and the challenges it faces.

Center 2: Adaptations for Survival

Assignment: Choose a world ecosystem and research the features of that ecosystem. Using your research, design a new creature that possesses specific adaptations that will allow it to survive and thrive in the ecosystem. Create an illustration, schematic, or model of your new creature with labeling and justification for the features and characteristics you have combined.

Arts Differentiation, Student Instructions:

- *Music:* Write and perform a song for your new creature highlighting the qualities that will make it thrive.
- *Drama:* Script and produce an interview between your new creature and the scientist who discovers it, another creature that lives in the ecosystem, or another relevant character. Highlight your attributes and your ability to thrive.
- *Art:* Create an evolutionary timeline showing the creature's development over time based upon influences in the ecosystem.
- *Dance:* How will your creature move? Create a jive, ballet, or tap dance representing the characteristics and movements of the creature.

Center 3: Life Cycles

Assignment: Create a life cycle book that defines and illustrates different types of life cycles (e.g., mammal, bird, metamorphosis, incomplete metamorphosis, complete metamorphosis). Choose 15 organisms and categorize them in your book with illustrations and captions.

Arts Differentiation, Student Instructions:

- *Music:* Find/perform or create/perform a life cycle song. Use different vocal qualities for each stage.

- *Drama:* Choose an organism that undergoes complete metamorphosis and create a monologue titled "The Story of My Life."
- *Art:* Create a three-dimensional model of a life cycle. Explain or label each stage.
- *Dance*: Create a jazz or modern dance that represents a complete metamorphosis.

Center 4: Animal Classification

Assignment: Work with a partner to create a game or activity that teaches others about the classes of animals and provides practice by testing their knowledge. Include the characteristics of each class, specific examples of each, and analysis strategies to classify other animals.

Arts Differentiation, Student Instructions:

- *Music:* Create an animal classification song that provides the characteristics and members of each class. Use musical elements to help provide auditory distinction between each of the classes.
- *Drama:* Write a scene between representatives of each animal class. It can be a debate, an argument, a contest, a student meeting all of the animal classes, or another scenario in which each animal gets to make its case to explain how it is alike and different from the other representatives.
- *Art:* Create a set of scientific illustrations that show the qualities that make up each animal class. Use a new media to create your illustrations.
- *Dance:* Use pantomime to "be" organisms from each class. Using only movement, illustrate the similarities and differences among members of the different classes.

Everyday Life Expert Plan: Content Area Differentiation

An important facet of multidisciplinary differentiation is the specific adjustment of performance criteria for individuals or groups of students based on their instructional needs. This differentiation often occurs in the context of an agenda in which students have opportunities to choose areas of interest for research while creating a common product to showcase content mastery.

Standard Addressed: ELA.CCR3: Conduct short as well as more sustained research projects based on focused questions, demonstrating understanding of the subject under investigation.

Everyday Life Expert Plan: North or South (Choose Three)		
Food, Diet, and Dining	Transportation and Communication	Clothing and Fashion
Education and Religion	Inventions, Production, and Manufacturing	Entertainment, Celebrations, and Society
Choose at least three of the areas in which to become an expert. Generate a set of questions you will need to answer to represent all facets of the category in the part of the U.S. you selected. Your information should reflect varied social levels and regions. Be sure you contrast the experiences of everyday people and those in the military for each of your categories.		

Figure 7.2. Potential areas of research.

Student Instructions: Decide whether you will be researching daily life in the North or in the South during the Civil War. Choose at least three areas in which you will become an expert.

Assignment: Students choose whether they are going to research Northern or Southern life and choose the facets of life they will research from the chart in Figure 7.2. After researching the daily life of the Civil War, students share their findings in a series of posters that address each of the chosen categories of daily life. The product allows students to integrate language arts standard ELA.CCR3 while improving research skills to present a written product with strong use of visual integration.

The rubric in Figure 7.3 reflects the performance standards used for assessing the products for most students. An easy way to use the same task to differentiate the product and process for a student identified gifted in visual arts would be to provide support for the student in the acquisition or improvement of skills in figure drawing using resources such as Angela Gair's (1992) *How to Draw and Paint People,* then add a row on the rubric to assess growth in that skill, as shown in Figure 7.4.

The same process could be used to address any appropriate skill area in visual and performing arts. Adding a presentation strand would be appropriate for a drama student (see Figure 7.5). The teacher and student(s) may determine a presentation/performance emphasis (e.g., presenting as a Northern or Southerner, as a newscaster, as a tour guide, as a time traveler) to give voice to the presentation and to help with characterization. Again, the content, process, and product are basically the same, but

	4–Exemplary	3–Adequate	2–Approaching	1–Minimal
Content	Each topic is addressed thoroughly; illustrations and captioning combine to clarify the significance of the topic to daily life; each topic reflects insightful understanding of the differences in lifestyle among the social classes/regions.	Each topic is addressed; some significance is established; illustrations and captioning effectively explain the facts about the topic; posters address some distinctions between social classes/regions.	Each topic has some information, but answers are not fully developed; illustrations and captioning are not used together to help the reader understand; information paints a picture of a single lifestyle for all.	Each topic is not addressed; no information or inaccurate information is available for some topics; little or no explanation for illustrated or listed facts.
Research Requirements	Meets research requirements; all resources documented; reflects combination of sources of information beyond Internet.	Meets research requirements; all resources documented.	Meets some research requirements; some resources documented.	Documentation is limited, inaccurate, and/or missing.
Organization	Illustration placement, captioning, and lettering guide the reader to a clear understanding of the content; ideas flow across the pages.	Illustration placement, captioning, and lettering are clearly organized and make sense.	Illustration placement, captioning, and lettering show basic organization; some elements are placed so that they do not support visual organization.	Illustration placement, captioning, and lettering appear disorganized or random; placement interferes with ability to process the information/make connections.
Accuracy and Correctness	Visual and print materials are accurately represented and contain no usage, spelling, or factual errors.	Visual and print materials are accurately represented and contain few usage, spelling, or factual errors.	Visual and print materials are basically correct but usage, spelling, and/or factual errors interfere with accuracy of communication.	Visual and print materials include usage, spelling, and/or factual errors that reflect inaccurate information or significant lack of awareness of conventions.
Visual Impact	Use of color, shape, lettering, negative space, placement, etc. is purposeful to effectively communicate information and draw the eye through the posters as communication tools.	Use of color, shape, lettering, negative space, placement, etc. is effective to communicate the information.	Use of color, shape, lettering, negative space, placement, etc. are not consistently used to communicate; some lapses in effectiveness.	Use of color, shape, lettering, negative space, placement, etc. are ineffective or appear random; visual impact does not enhance the ability of the posters to communicate.

Figure 7.3. Daily life poster rubric.

	4–Exemplary	3–Adequate	2–Approaching	1–Minimal
Figure Drawing	Figures are correctly proportioned; figures are placed in varied positions and reflect appropriate depth and perspective; figures reflect varied body types and characters.	Figures are correctly proportioned; limited variety of positions employed; depth and perspective are appropriate; basic body type is represented.	Figures are not all correctly proportioned; figures appear as caricatures or repeated figures; limited awareness of depth and perspective.	Proportion is not addressed in human figures; production strategies are not representational.

Figure 7.4. Daily life poster rubric differentiated for visual art.

	4–Exemplary	3–Adequate	2–Approaching	1–Minimal
Characterization Oral Presentation	Vocal quality, voice and tone enhance character; vocal and facial expression enhances understanding and character development; gestures and movement enhance character development; volume, eye contact, and fluency enhance understanding.	Vocal quality is adequate to establish a character; some effective use of gestures and movement; volume, eye contact, and fluency are adequate.	Some effort is evident, but vocal quality, voice, and tone are inconsistently applied to establish character; limited or ineffective use of gestures and movement to establish character; volume, eye contact, and fluency inconsistently used to establish character.	Vocal quality, voice, and tone are not addressed to establish character; use of gestures and movement is not present to establish character; character volume, eye contact, and fluency reflect limited knowledge and preparation.

Figure 7.5. Daily life poster rubric differentiated for performing arts.

the presentation of the product for the gifted drama student would reflect an additional set of expectations and guidance toward improved skills in presentation as a character. By providing guidance and access to a resource such as Friedman's (2002) *Break a Leg! The Kid's Guide to Acting and Stagecraft*, students can then be provided opportunities to apply those skills in multidisciplinary activities.

Sharing the rubric with students ahead of time is essential to establishing criteria for success. As students know the qualities on which their performance will be assessed, it is easier for them to self-assess based on their progress, and it will be easier for students to internalize the performance standards related to their fields of talent.

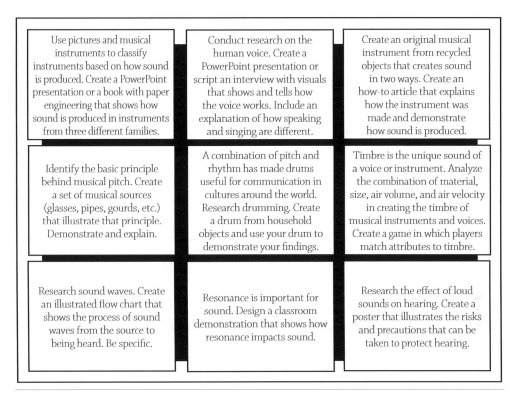

Figure 7.6. Sound bits Think-Tac-Toe.

Science: Process/Product Differentiation

Music and dance have direct links to science standards, providing a natural connection for multidisciplinary differentiation. Agendas and centers designed to address specific science standards can easily be adapted to provide diagnostic attention to skill development in the arts.

Standards Addressed: NSES Physical Science B: Students should develop an understanding that sound is produced by vibrations; the pitch of sound is varied by changing the rate of vibration; the position and motion of objects can be changed by pushing or pulling; and the size of the change is related to the strength of the push or pull; NA.K-4. 1. Students sing independently, on pitch and in rhythm, with appropriate timbre, diction, and posture, and maintain a steady tempo.

Planning around concepts within NSES Standard Physical Science B readily supports differentiation of content, process, and product.

Differentiating the agenda in Figure 7.6 for a student gifted in vocal music can be addressed through the National Standards for Art Education music standard NA.K-4.1. A task can easily be superimposed on the Think-Tac-Toe board and assigned in combination with the others chosen by the student (see Figure 7.7). Criteria for

> Record your own voice singing a
> well-known selection. Change each
> variable for sound production—
> volume of air, velocity of air, posture,
> etc. and record again. Analyze
> your performance and identify
> the combination that resulted in
> the best sound. Summarize.

Figure 7.7. Sound bits Think-Tac-Toe differentiated for vocal music.

success are established prior to completion of the task so the student is aware of the growth goal for the activity. Follow-up questions will focus on student findings, teacher analysis of the recordings with feedback, and goal-setting to incorporate findings into vocal practice and performance.

Linking the science standards relating to sound and motion makes it possible to design stations and activities that can address physical science concepts and musical instruments as simple machines. Stations provide activities and potential for differentiation for students with high potential in the arts.

Center 1: The Body as a Machine

Assignment: After reviewing the simple machines, students should analyze the human body and identify the simple machines represented in the muscular and skeletal systems (i.e., lever, fulcrum, wedge, inclined plane). Then, they can present their analysis as a poster series, a PowerPoint presentation, a science TV segment, or use another strategy negotiated with the teacher.

Arts Differentiation, Student Instructions:

- *Music:* Listen to Robin Walling's "The Bones Song" or an original bone song that identifies major bones and their functions. Perform the song for the class. Add instrumentation that supports the sounds and mood appropriate to the subject of the song.
- *Drama:* Develop a monologue as the skeletal system to tell about your functions, your construction, and the simple machines within the human body. Present your monologue in costume or with a skeleton puppet.
- *Art:* Research the symbolism of skeletons in art among various cultures. Create a piece of artwork that symbolizes the skeleton's importance to survival.
- *Dance:* Review existing skeleton dances such as Miley Cyrus' "Bone Dance" or Jenny Fixman's "Bones." Learn the dance or create an original dance repre-

senting the skeletal system, the connections, and the functions. Present and/or teach your dance to the class.

Center 2: Simple Machines

Assignment: Students will create an illustrated picture book of at least eight of the simple machines. They should include a schematic or flow chart for each machine that shows the steps in energy transfer that occur as the machine works. For an advanced assignment, students can keep a simple machine diary for 24 hours, illustrating their diary to show the simple machines used and how each works. At the end of the 24 hours, they should analyze the role of simple machines in their life and write a position article that identifies the simple machine(s) that they find most important in daily life.

Arts Differentiation, Student Instructions:

- *Music:* Listen to Bill Nye's "Simple Machines" and other musical settings of simple machine information. Choose one of those or create an original simple machine song. Use existing or original instruments to orchestrate your song, identifying the simple machines in each.
- *Drama:* Create an award for the most important simple machine. Write the nomination speech and present it using effective public speaking strategies.
- *Art:* Using Mark Hiner's (1986) *Paper Engineering for Pop-Up Books and Cards* as a guide, create a pop-up book of simple machines. Identify each simple machine that is utilized in the paper engineering. Conduct an oral reflection with the teacher regarding the media and trial-and-error processes used to create the effects achieved.
- *Dance:* Research dance and simple machines. Read Kenneth Laws' (2008) *Physics and the Art of Dance: Understanding Movement.* Create a set of at least five movement stations in which the body illustrates the actions of simple machines such as lever, inclined plane, wedge, screw, pulley, wheel and axle, and fulcrum. You may use props. Write a task card for each station that explains the movement and the simple machine it illustrates. Demonstrate and guide other students in those same movements.

Center 3: Force and Motion

Assignment: Students should read Denyse O'Leary's (2011) *What Are Newton's Laws of Motion?* That information and additional research on force and motion will be used to design a set of experiments that use simple machines to demonstrate the results of change of energy and force. Students conduct their experiments, record their results, and publish their findings through a booklet or PowerPoint presentation.

Arts Differentiation, Student Instructions:

- *Music:* Listen to Jack Hartman's "Force" in hip-hop style. Select another vocal style (e.g., ballad, folk, rock, pop, opera, blues), and convert the song to the new style. Write a reflection on the musical changes that were required to change the style. Perform your new version.

- *Drama:* Read John Kreng's (2007) *Fight Choreography: The Art of Non-Verbal Dialogue*. Select and choreograph a fight sequence with a partner. Videotape the final version, then add a stop-motion or slow-motion section that demonstrates the laws of motion in each step of the sequence.

- *Art:* Use Stykz 1.0.2 or other animation software to create animated demonstrations of the laws of motion. Include voiceover or print captioning to explain the laws and the impact of changing the amount of force, location, or other variables.

- *Dance:* Analyze a video of a favorite dance to identify the laws of motion in practice and the changes that occur as force and position are changed. Evaluate the aesthetic impact of the changes in the movement. Present your findings orally or in a written format. Use visuals.

Each center listed above can be readily converted to a multiactivity agenda, depending on the teacher's goals for individual students and the time frame available.

RECOMMENDED RESOURCES

Classroom teachers committed to successful implementation of multidisciplinary and arts differentiation need access to some fundamental resources. Ideally, the most important resources will be building- and district-level arts experts. The school music teacher, band director, and art teacher can be vital experts in locating classroom resources and helping with the development of discipline-specific skill sequences and the identification of professionally accurate mastery criteria. Individuals in the community with similar areas of expertise can also be critical to arts implementation in the classroom.

Resources available from national arts organizations must be referenced at the school and classroom level in order to assure accurate standards implementation in the arts. Each of the national arts organizations—National Association for Music Education (NAME), National Art Education Association (NAEA), American Alliance for Theatre and Education (AATE), and National Dance Education Organization (NDEO)—provides developmentally appropriate standards for students, recommendations for experiences and instruction at all grade levels, and resources to assist in implementing those standards.

Print and media resources are also essential for both teachers and students in a quality multidisciplinary program, as a differentiated classroom will reflect a variety of student needs that cannot be met from a single textbook or source. Recommended general resources are included at the end of the chapter. Many of the listed resources include outstanding bibliographies that reference additional excellent resources.

PUTTING IT ALL TOGETHER—FUNDAMENTALS OF EFFECTIVE DIFFERENTIATION

Preassessment

The complexity of designing effective multidisciplinary and arts differentiation has been addressed through attention to fundamental practices. The first is preassessment. What do the students know? For each standard and skill set, preassessment is essential in order to determine the levels of student readiness and need for the content to be learned, for it is impractical for us to teach a student something she already knows. Specific preassessments are not included in this chapter because the multidisciplinary activities are deliberately designed to depend on a level of prior knowledge and extend the applications. Although preassessments are not included, it is imperative that the teacher have accurate knowledge of students' content knowledge, skill readiness, and interests in order to design and implement activities at the appropriate level of challenge.

Clear Mastery Criteria

The second essential for effective multidisciplinary differentiation is clear expectations regarding mastery criteria. Based upon the instructional standards, what will success look like? Although effective instructional design requires high expectations for all students, adjustments in those criteria facilitate differentiation. Operating under a common set of standards, it is possible to adjust the emphasis for mastery to provide a best match for students presenting with different interests, needs, and abilities. In a multidisciplinary, arts-based differentiation, the range of expectations can be readily expanded to address high levels of content knowledge and application in the context of a continuum of standards-based competencies in the arts.

Differentiation of Content, Process, or Product

Once decisions have been made about what students need to know or be able to do as a result of the instructional sequence, multidisciplinary centers and agendas can facilitate differentiation by providing formats for adjustment of content, or what information the student will access and apply; process, or how the student will access information and resources and how they will apply them to new learning; and product, or the measurable performance of the student to demonstrate learning.

Any standard and set of learning targets can be differentiated in all three ways. By using a standard that applies across all grade levels, the process is demonstrated as follows.

Standard addressed: History standard: European exploration and colonization resulted in cultural and ecological interactions among previously unconnected peoples.

Learning Targets: (1) Students will identify purposes and outcomes of European exploration in North America and related conflicts. (2) Students will analyze cultural impacts on each group as a result of interactions between European explorers and settlers and the Native Americans. (3) Students will evaluate the beliefs each group held about the other and the impact of those beliefs on actions.

Common Content/Process/Product Assignment: All students read the social studies textbook and answer the exploration and colonization questions.

Common Content/Differentiated Process and Product Assignment: All students read the social studies textbook. Students who demonstrate mastery of the basic content read a related chapter in Joy Hakim's (2007) *Making Thirteen Colonies*. Using both sources and additional research, students will create an explorer-Native American graphic that shows purposes, conflicts, and outcomes for each major European power that settled in North America. Graphic information will be presented through a poster series, cause and effect flow charts, or PowerPoint presentation. Information may be written in script form (e.g., dialogue, monologue, or interview format) and supported with visuals.

Differentiated Content/Common Process/Differentiated Product Assignment: Students will choose a European power in the Age of Exploration. All students will research the purposes of exploration and colonization, the conflicts created in the process, and the outcomes of exploration using a minimum of two print and two electronic sources. Students will choose to present their research findings (1) as a representative of the colonizing group through a monologue or dialogue; (2) through a cause-and-effect article for "The Explorer Times"; (3) as member of a debate panel on the topic "Exploration—Riches or Ravaging"; or (4) in a product determined in consultation with the teacher.

By matching the level and type of differentiation to the needs of students, teachers increase student engagement and tasks become more authentic to the interests and abilities of individuals

Authentic Assessment

The final critical attribute of a successful differentiated learning sequence is authentic assessment based on clearly identified mastery criteria built into the instruction and product development. In a well-designed lesson, those mastery criteria are clearly articulated to students through the learning targets and product decisions and are diagnostically matched to students' needs and abilities in order to reflect growth goals. Differentiated rubrics are a logical tool for making product/performance assessment authentic. Through multidisciplinary differentiation and differentiation in the arts, simple adjustments to the rubric that address targeted skills allow for content, process, and product assessment.

FINAL THOUGHTS

Throughout the chapter, examples of differentiation of each facet of the instructional sequence have illustrated the flexibility and instructional choices inherent in the process. Although few teachers differentiate every task for every student, the range of student interests, needs, and abilities in every classroom makes purposeful differentiation a necessity in meeting the goal of helping all children progress at their optimum rates. Through multidisciplinary differentiation with an emphasis on integration of the arts, education can play a vital role perpetuating the creativity, imagination, and vision that will continue to make this world a better place!

CHAPTER 7 RESOURCES

Bones, Jennifer Fixman—http://www.songsforteaching.com/jennyfixmanedutunes/bones.htm

The Bone Dance—http://www.youtube.com/watch?v=ZGdK4T7WUrA&feature=related

The Bones Song, Teaching the Bones of the Human Body, Robin Walling—http://www.songsforteaching.com/scienceinsong/206bones.htm

Fun Dance Moves: How to learn the Bone Dance—http://www.youtube.com/watch?v=TcgY9DQ4J8o&feature=fvwrel

Levers in the Human Body—http://www.dynamicscience.com.au/tester/solutions/hydraulicus/humanbody.htm

Skeleton Dance Costumes—http://www.youtube.com/watch?v=gsS3twXiJL4&feature=fvsr

The Skeletal System—http://www.youtube.com/watch?v=vya4wpS2fgk

Skeletal System Resource—http://www.healthline.com/human-body-maps/skeletal-system

American Alliance for Theatre and Education. (2000). *National standards for theatre education.* Bethesda, MD: Author.

Gilbert, A. G. (2000). *Teaching the three R's through movement experiences.* Seattle, WA: University of Washington.

Levy, G. (2005). *112 acting games: A comprehensive workbook of theatre games for developing acting skills.* Colorado Springs, CO: Meriweather Publishing.

McPherson, G. (2006). *The child as musician: A handbook of musical development.* New York, NY: Oxford University Press.

Mirus, J., White, E., Bucek, L., & Paulson, P. (1996). *Dance education initiative curriculum guide.* Golden Valley, MN: Perpich Center for Arts Education.

National Art Education Association. (1994). *National visual arts standards.* Reston, VA: Author.

National Center for History in the Schools. (1996). *National standards for history.* Los Angeles, CA: NCHS Press.

National Dance Education Organization. (2002). *Standards for a K–12 model program: Opportunities to learn in dance arts education.* Silver Springs, MD: Author.

Page, N. (1996). *Music as a way of knowing.* Portland, ME: Stenhouse.

Spolin, V. (1986). *Theatre games for the classroom: A teacher's handbook.* Evanston, IL: Northwestern University Press.

Stewart, M. (1997). *Thinking through aesthetics.* Worcester, MA: Davis.

Worley, B. (2006). Differentiation in the arts: What does this mean? *Understanding Our Gifted, 18,* 3–5.

REFERENCES

Bridges, R. (1999). *Through my eyes.* New York, NY: Scholastic.

Bridges, R. (2009). *Ruby Bridges goes to school: My true story.* New York, NY: Scholastic.

Coles, R. (1995). *The story of Ruby Bridges.* New York, NY: Scholastic.

Consortium of National Arts Education Associations. (1994). *National standards for arts education: What every young American should know and be able to do in the arts.* Lanham, MD: Rowman & Littlefield.

Friedman, L. (2002). *Break a leg! The kid's guide to acting and stagecraft.* New York, NY: Workman.

Gair, A. (1992). *How to draw and paint people (Art for children).* London, England: Booksales.

Hakim, J. (2007). *Making thirteen colonies: 1600–1740. A history of US book 2.* New York, NY: Oxford University Press.

Hiner, M. (1986). *Paper engineering for pop-up books and cards.* Miami, FL: Parkwest Publications.

Kreng, J. (2007). *Fight choreography: The art of non-verbal dialogue.* Boston, MA: Thomson Course Technology PTR.

Laws, K. (2008). *Physics and the art of dance: Understanding movement.* New York, NY: Oxford University Press.

National Governors Association, & Council of Chief State School Officers. (2010). *Common core state standards: Key points of the English language arts standards.* Retrieved from http://www.corestandards.org/about-the-standards/key-points-in-english-language-arts

National Research Council. (1996). *National science education standards.* Washington, DC: National Academy Press.

O'Leary, D. (2011). *What are Newton's laws of motion?* New York, NY: Crabtree.

Chapter 8

Making Differentiation Through Centers Manageable

Julia Link Roberts and Julia Roberts Boggess

The biggest mistake of past centuries in teaching has been to treat all children as if they were variants of the same individual and thus to feel justified in teaching them all the same subjects in the same way.

—Howard Gardner

A teacher may say, "Differentiating through learning centers sounds good, but how do you make it work?" That is an important question. The teacher must have a plan in place to make the instructional management work when students are engaged in more than one learning experience—likely multiple learning experiences. And the plan must be simple—in fact, the simpler, the better.

START THE YEAR DIFFERENTIATING

In Chapter 2, teachers are urged to differentiate early on in the year. On Day 1 of the school year, the teacher needs to discuss the range of interests and experiences among the students. The teacher needs to highlight those differences by identifying the levels of interests and skills in swimming, running long distances, playing an instrument, using an iPad, or discussing science fiction (just to name a few possibilities—teachers should come up with others that fit their students). Likewise, students could share their favorite foods, books, movie seen this summer, number of cousins, number of houses lived in, and so forth. Such a discussion will lead students to recognize the wide variety of interests represented in the class, as well as the interests they share with others in the class. A great way for teachers to figure out major interests is to have students write about how they spend their time when not in school. Writing is important as the teacher has a record of the individual student's interests. Good classroom management starts with knowing one's students.

SIMPLIFY

A way to make differentiating with centers work well is to simplify. One way to simplify is to establish procedures that must be followed when students work at their centers. What are the procedures that lead to independent learning? For example, begin working in centers as a class to allow for detailed instruction of all directions and expectations. It is best to start off with only 2–3 centers at a time. Teachers can add additional centers once students have shown that they can work effectively and independently in centers.

All students must know what to do. They must know the routine. They need to know what to do if they need assistance. If students are working in a group, perhaps the teacher can identify an "expert" for each center, so students know whom to ask for help while the teacher is working with other groups. Where does the student leave work that is not yet finished and where does he file the finished product?

Instructions for centers must be specific and easy to understand. Expectations must be spelled out. For example, voices at centers should not be heard beyond the next person; for elementary children, the request may be to use "6-inch voices."

Another example of a way to simplify is to use a protocol—a plan or procedure that will work in many situations. For example, the DAP Tool (Roberts & Inman, 2009) is a protocol to guide students in the development of a product and to assist the teacher in the assessment of the product. Having a protocol also makes it possible to offer options with products if the student(s) suggests substituting a product for the one the teacher offers. A file of DAP Tools can serve as a ready reference for a student choosing to work on a product on his own or with a cluster of classmates. He may select the tier of the DAP Tool that will allow him to advance in his skill and experience with a specific product. A protocol makes it possible to establish priorities that make it clear to students just what they need to do in order to have a high-quality product.

PREASSESSMENT AS AN ONGOING STRATEGY

Decisions about readiness should be made based on preassessment for a particular unit. Those decisions are reconsidered as the topic changes and new units are planned. Preassessment is similar to taking the temperature of a child, which will differ on different days. Preassessment is the reading of the child's temperature related to what she knows about the topic, skills needed for the next unit, and interests in the upcoming study. A student may know a lot about one topic in social studies but have no experience with another. Students need opportunities to learn with others who are equally interested in a particular topic. All students benefit from opportunities to learn with idea-mates who may or may not be age-mates—others who share their interests.

GROUPING BY INTERESTS, READINESS, AND/OR LEARNING PREFERENCES

Effective management of students can often be accomplished by grouping for instructional purposes. Of course, the teacher sets growth goals for each student in the class. If the teacher groups for readiness, he has assessment data to guide him in making instructional decisions as he forms groups for a particular unit. He groups students by what they know about the topic of the unit and/or the requisite skills that students can demonstrate.

Instructions for individuals or small groups can be provided through centers or agendas. Instruction that is too easy leads to boredom and diminished interest in the topic being studied. Instruction that is too hard leads to frustration and also to loss of interest. Flexible grouping facilitates learning at high levels.

Interests about a particular topic can provide another way to form instructional groups. For example, a class studying nutrition could be grouped by student interest in learning about different aspects of the topic. Some students may be most interested in advertising and its effects on nutrition. What foods are advertised most frequently, and how nutritious are those foods? Graphs with explanations could be the final products. Another group may have expressed more interest in planning meals that are both nutritious and well balanced. Their final product could be a week of menus. Still another cluster of students would prefer to write a children's book to teach younger children about good nutrition. All students are learning about nutrition, but they are working in groupings that were formed by their interests and learning preferences.

Multiple products provide multiple pathways to learn the same concept. Interest is often generated by choice of products. Everyone learns about the content being studied, and all contribute to the overall learning in the class by sharing and discussing what has been learned.

RESOURCES

The major management question with differentiating is "How do you arrange resources to maximize learning for all students?" Resources include print resources, digital resources, and human resources. Print resources on a topic can be available at the various reading levels that match students in the center. One could read about cells at a science center that contains elementary-level books through high school and college biology texts. What makes a particular resource appropriate is the appropriate level of challenge that it provides for the student who is the reader. When all students can read at a level of challenge (but not too much challenge) about a topic or concept being studied, all students learn and all can enter any discussion held about that topic.

Professionals in an area can be interviewed as primary sources or be available to provide their expertise. Volunteers can also be useful resources to be used in myriad ways in the classroom to facilitate centers.

One other valuable resource for the teacher is the *NAGC Pre-K–Grade 12 Gifted Programming Standards* (National Association for Gifted Children, 2010) document. These standards are especially powerful because they focus on student outcomes. What will the students be doing when these standards are implemented?

RECORD KEEPING

Students, even young students, can manage their own work in centers. Teachers need to place a file in a location that is accessible to students. The file will store student work being done in centers. Each student will have a tab in the file. For young students, it is important to model how to file final products and other assessments completed at the centers.

The preassessment itself is an important record. Comparing the preassessment results with later learning or the postassessment documents learning progress. These records are valuable when communicating with parents about the individual child and also in explaining why not all children in a class are completing the same assignments on the same time schedule. After all, their levels of readiness, interests, and learning profiles are different.

CONCLUDING COMMENTS

Classrooms in which differentiation is standard practice are well planned, and both procedures and expectations are thoroughly understood by children and young people. Students are engaged in learning, and they are working as individuals and in small groups. Groupings are flexible and reflect readiness, interests, and/or learning profiles. The teacher has a system for recording progress and communicates learning progress to children as well as to parents. Resources are carefully managed and as plentiful as possible. Such a classroom is one in which each child engages in appropriately challenging learning opportunities. Expectations are high, and children work hard to reach their learning goals. There is no learning ceiling for children.

Centers denote a place in the classroom, and the same means of differentiation that is associated with centers can be accomplished with agendas in a classroom without enough space to designate centers.

REFERENCES

National Association for Gifted Children. (2010). *NAGC Pre-K–Grade 12 Gifted Education Programming Standards: A blueprint for quality gifted education programs.* Washington, DC: Author.

Roberts, J. L., & Inman, T. F. (2009). *Strategies for differentiating instruction: Best practices for the classroom* (2nd ed.). Waco, TX: Prufrock Press.

Chapter 9

Concluding Thoughts and Next Steps

Julia Link Roberts and Julia Roberts Boggess

*Give a man a fish and you feed him for a day. Teach a
man to fish and you feed him for a lifetime.*

—Chinese Proverb

As the proverb states, this book is intended to help teachers "learn how to fish" or, rather, how to begin to use centers or how to improve and enhance their use of centers as a strategy to engage students in learning. Teachers must keep in mind that the goal for all children, including those who are gifted and talented, is to become lifelong learners. Doing so will make it possible for children to reach their potential and for our society to benefit from them becoming artists, scientists, mathematicians, social scientists, mothers and fathers, community leaders, innovators, entrepreneurs, and anything else they choose to become.

All children deserve opportunities to have learning that is worth their time and effort. The work must be at an appropriate level of challenge. The appropriate level of challenge requires effort to reach that learning goal, but the goal must be at an academic level that is reachable for individual students. Those levels will seldom be the same for an entire class, even if it is a class of advanced learners. Excellence is the target, as expectations are high for all students.

Differentiation is the overall strategy that will allow all children to make appropriate continuous progress. Teachers need to find other teachers interested in differentiating and plan with them. They can form study groups to look at differentiation and learn about various strategies for effectively differentiating. As they implement differentiation strategies and their students flourish, other teachers will begin to ask questions and express interest.

Another way to learn more about differentiation and gifted children is to study and use the *NAGC Pre-K–Grade 12 Gifted Education Programming Standards* (National

Association for Gifted Children, 2010) document, which can be accessed at http://nagc.org. Another useful resource is the book *NAGC Pre-K–Grade 12 Gifted Education Programming Standards: A Guide to Planning and Implementing High-Quality Services* (Johnsen, 2012), which examines the standards and describes implementation strategies.

The key is to start small and differentiate a unit of study or create a differentiated learning center. A teacher cannot go from little or no differentiation to differentiating all learning experiences; that is unrealistic. A strategy that is likely to lead to success is to start with what is manageable and build a repertoire of strategies that work together to have a classroom in which children are learning about the same topic or concept but at paces and levels of readiness that incorporate interests and learning preferences.

The goal for schools is for students to learn. Fourth-, fifth-, and sixth-grade students gave the following responses when asked "How do you know when you are learning?" Responses included:

- I start to build questions in my head.
- If I get a question wrong or someone disagrees with me.
- I can explain what I know to others.
- I make a (~~misteak~~) mistake and I learn from it.
- I find a new way to solve a problem.
- I want to know more.
- I see things from a different point of view.
- I visualize it and absorb what I'm learning.

Learning is so much more than having right answers. Students who are learning on an ongoing basis are exactly what differentiation is all about. Happy differentiating to teachers everywhere!

REFERENCES

Johnsen, S. K. (Ed.). (2012). *NAGC Pre-K–Grade 12 Gifted Education Programming Standards: A guide to planning and implementing high-quality services*. Waco, TX: Prufrock Press.

National Association for Gifted Children (2010). *NAGC Pre-K–Grade 12 Gifted Education Programming Standards: A blueprint for quality gifted education programs*. Washington, DC: Author.

About the Editors

Julia Link Roberts, Ed.D., is the Mahurin Professor of Gifted Studies at Western Kentucky University. She is the Executive Director of The Center for Gifted Studies and the Carol Martin Gatton Academy of Mathematics and Science in Kentucky. Dr. Roberts was honored with the 2011 Acorn Award as the outstanding professor at a 4-year college or university in Kentucky and with the 2011 William Nallia Educational Leadership Award from the Kentucky Association of School Administrators. She is a member of the Executive Committee of the World Council for Gifted and Talented Children and a board member of The Association for the Gifted (a division of the Council for Exceptional Children) and the Kentucky Association for Gifted Education. She is coauthor with Julia Roberts Boggess of *Teacher's Survival Guide: Gifted Education*. She is coauthor with Tracy Ford Inman of *Strategies for Differentiating Instruction: Best Practices for the Classroom* (2009 Legacy Award winner for the outstanding book for educators in gifted education by the Texas Association for the Gifted and Talented) and *Assessing Differentiated Student Products: A Protocol for Development and Evaluation*. Dr. Roberts directs summer and Saturday programs for children and young people who are gifted and talented. Dr. Roberts and her husband Richard live in Bowling Green, KY. They have two daughters, Stacy Moots and Julie Boggess, and four grand-girls, Elizabeth, Caroline, Jane Ann, and Claire.

Julia Roberts Boggess is an elementary librarian at Pearre Creek Elementary School in Williamson County, TN. She has taught in the primary grades and served as a gifted resource teacher. In 2008, Mrs. Boggess was awarded an $8,000 Jenny's Heroes grant from the Jenny Jones Foundation. She has taught drama and literature to elementary and middle school students in Saturday and summer programs offered by The Center for Gifted Studies at Western Kentucky University. She coauthored *Teacher's Survival Guide: Gifted Education* with Julia Link Roberts. Mrs. Boggess earned a bachelor's degree in elementary education, a master's degree in elementary education with an endorsement in gifted education, and a master's degree in library media education at Western Kentucky University. She lives in Franklin, TN, with her husband, Mark, and her 3-year-old daughter, Claire.

About the Authors

Martha M. Day, Ed.D., is assistant professor of science education at Western Kentucky University. She serves as Executive Director of GSKyTeach and Co-Director of SKyTeach, programs that are part of a national initiative led by the National Mathematics and Science Initiative to improve teacher quality in the STEM disciplines. Dr. Day is a frequent presenter at national conferences on topics related to inquiry-based instruction, project-based learning, increasing cognitive complexity in assessments, and content-area literacy. She also trains school leaders and teachers in mentoring and coaching beginning teachers. Dr. Day has 15 years of K–12 teaching and administrative experience in urban school settings. Her current research and writing focuses on 5E inquiry science activities for the science classroom.

Tracy Ford Inman, Ed.D., is associate director of The Center for Gifted Studies at Western Kentucky University and active on the state, national, and international levels in gifted education. She has taught English at the high school and collegiate levels, as well as in summer programs for gifted and talented youth. In addition to writing and co-writing several articles, Tracy has coauthored two books with Julia Link Roberts published by Prufrock Press: *Strategies for Differentiating Instruction: Best Practices for the Classroom*, now in its second edition, and *Assessing Differentiated Student Products: A Protocol for Development and Evaluation*. Tracy and Julia received the 2009 Legacy Book Award from the Texas Association for the Gifted and Talented for *Strategies for Differentiating Instruction*. Tracy was coeditor of *Parenting Gifted Children: The Authoritative Guide From the National Association for Gifted Children*, a compilation of the best articles in *Parenting for High Potential*, which won the Legacy Book Award in 2011.

Jana Kirchner, Ph.D., is a Social Studies and Literacy Consultant for the Green River Regional Educational Cooperative in Bowling Green, KY. Dr. Kirchner has 22 years of experience in education that includes teaching high school history and English, serving as Social Studies Department Head/Curriculum Coordinator, teaching as an Instructor/Practitioner in Western Kentucky University's Teacher Education department, and serving as Executive Director of the Kentucky Council for Social Studies. She earned her Ph.D. in educational leadership (with an emphasis on curriculum and instruction) from the University of Louisville.

Jan W. Lanham, Ph.D., has worked in the field of education in a variety of roles: fine arts teacher (music and art), choral director, gifted education teacher and coordinator, classroom teacher at all levels, instructor in secondary and middle school gifted camps, teacher/coordinator of gifted enrichment experiences, author of curriculum materials, and adjunct university instructor. She balances her current role as elementary principal with her involvement with gifted and exceptional education at the local, state, and national level. She and her husband, Kevin, are the proud parents of three sons.

Janet Lynne Tassell, Ph.D., an assistant professor in the School of Teacher Education at Western Kentucky University, was the recipient of the college's Teaching Award. Specializing in mathematics education and gifted education, Dr. Tassell has taken her experience as a mathematics teacher and as Director of Learning and Assessment for a rural school district, and brought her unique skills to WKU. She is the Director of the Toyota Math and Technology Leadership Academy and serves as the Professional Development Director for the Javits-funded GEMS grant/initiative for elementary mathematics and science. She is a contributing author in *The Peak in the Middle* and an associate editor for *School Science and Mathematics*.